contents

iv **Preface**
by Michael DeMarco, M.A.

CHAPTERS

12 **Yagi Meitatsu Discusses the Not-So-Secret Techniques of Okinawan Goju-ryu Karate**
by Robert Toth

15 **Steve Arneil and the British Kyokushinkai: An Interview**
by Graham Noble

47 **The Legacy of Dr. Richard Kim: An Interview with Brian Ricci**
by Robert Toth

64 **George Dillman and the Influences in Pressure Point Theory and Practice**
by Peter Hobart, J.D.

75 **The Stories of Meibukan Goju-ryu Karate as Told by Yagi Meitatsu**
by Robert Toth

94 **Politics and Karate: Historical Influences on the Practice of Goju-ryu**
by Giles Hopkins, M.A.

120 **Evaluating Makiwara Punching Board Performance**
by Paul K. Smith, Ph.D., Timothy Niiler, Ph.D., and Peter McCullough, B.S.

130 **Attention, Sit, Meditate, Bow, Ready Position: Ritualized Dojo Pattern or Character Training?**
by Marvin Labbate

142 **Issues Concerning Board Breaking**
by Phil Davison, M.A.

150 **Ryukyu Kempo and Small Circle Jujitsu**
by Will Higginbotham, B.A.

154 **Kata-based Training of Goju-ryu Karate**
by Marvin Labbate

158 **Tekko: Ryukyu Kobudo Shinkokai's Knuckle Duster**
by Mario McKenna, M.Sc.

162 **Index**

preface

What would you like to obtain from your research and practice of an Okinawan martial art? For an academic, it would be to obtain historical and cultural facts and details. For a practitioner, it would be to gain expertise in the combative skills. If you're interested in both, this third of a three-volume anthology is assembled for your convenience to facilitate your endeavors. These volumes assemble a wealth of material originally published during the two decades when the *Journal of Asian Martial Arts* was in print.

Hundreds of pages and photographs present the richness of Okinawan martial traditions, from the original combatives to those influenced by Chinese and mainland Japanese martial art styles. The variety of topics shown in the table of contents indicate the depth and breath in the chapters, along with the authors who are well-known for their meticulous research and practical skills in specific arts.

These three volumes dive deep into the history and culture of Okinawan martial arts. You'll find coverage of the actual artifacts—the material culture related to weaponry and training methods. Instructions from the masters details both open-hand techniques as well as with weapons. The chapters offer insights into the lives of many masters over the past few centuries, giving the *raison d'être* for these unique fighting arts—their reason for being.

Many streams of arts have contributed to the martial traditions found on the small island: Naha-*te*, Shuri-*te*, Fukien White Crane, Shorin, Goju, Motobu, Shotokan, Isshin, Kyokushin, Pwang Gai Noon, Shito, Uechi, and the list continues. . .

Along with the various styles come the associated training methods, such as conditioning exercises with weights and creatively designed apparatus, such as the punching post (*makiwara*), or stone lever and stone padlock-shaped weights. Some become battle-hardened by active and passive breaking of objects (*tameshiwari*), including wooden boards, baseball bats, rocks, and ice. The extensive use of weaponry is found in many Okinawan styles, often associated with their farming and fishing occupations.

Such a blend of history and culture make the Okinawan fighting traditions a fascinating field of study. Besides being such vital sources of information, these three volumes will prove enjoyable reading and permanent at-hand reference sources in your library.

Michael A. DeMarco, Publisher
Santa Fe, New Mexico
January 2017

Okinawan Vol. 3
Martial Traditions

te, tode, karate, karatedo, kobudo

沖縄手

An Anthology of Articles from the *Journal of Asian Martial Arts*
Compiled by Michael A. DeMarco, M.A.

Disclaimer
Please note that the authors and publisher of this book are not responsible in any manner whatsoever for any injury that may result from practicing the techniques and/or following the instructions given within. Since the physical activities described herein may be too strenuous in nature for some readers to engage in safely, it is essential that a physician be consulted prior to training.

All Rights Reserved
No part of this publication, including illustrations, may be reproduced or utilized in any form or by any means, electronic or mechanical, including photocopying, recording, or by any information storage and retrieval system (beyond that copying permitted by sections 107 and 108 of the US Copyright Law and except by reviewers for the public press), without written permission from Via Media Publishing Company.

Warning: Any unauthorized act in relation to a copyright work may result in both a civil claim for damages and criminal prosecution.

Copyright © 2017 by Via Media Publishing Company
941 Calle Mejia #822, Santa Fe, NM 87501 USA

All articles in this anthology were originally published in the *Journal of Asian Martial Arts*. Listed according to the table of contents for this anthology:

Toth, R. (2004), Vol. 13 No. 4, pp. 60-71
Noble, G. (2005), Vol. 14, No. 1, pp. 52-73
Toth, R. (2006), Vol. 15, No. 1, pp. 62-75
Hobart, P. (2006), Vol. 15, No. 2, pp. 50-59
Toth, R. (2007), Vol. 16 No. 2, pp. 48-61
Hopkins, G. (2007), Vol. 16 No. 3, pp. 30-49
Smith, P., Niiler, T., & McCullough, P. (2010), Vol. 19 No. 2, pp. 34-45
Labbate, M. (2011), Vol. 20 No. 1, pp. 82-93
Davison, P. (2011), Vol. 20 No. 3, pp. 22-31
Higginbotham, W. (2012). In *Asian Martial Arts:
Constructive Thoughts & Practical Applications*, pp. 70-73
Labbate, M. (2012). In *Asian Martial Arts:
Constructive Thoughts & Practical Applications*, pp. 98-101
McKenna, M. (2012). In *Asian Martial Arts:
Constructive Thoughts & Practical Applications*, pp. 110-113

Book and cover design by
Via Media Publishing Company

Edited by Michael A. DeMarco, M.A.

Cover illustration
Artistic interpretation of Funakoshi Gichin (1868-1957), the founder of Shotokan Karate-Do. © Illustration by Feodor Tamarsky • www.tamarskygallery.com
ISBN: 9781893765429

www.viamediapublishing.com

chapter 1

Yagi Meitatsu Discusses the Not-So-Secret Techniques of Okinawan Goju-ryu Karate

by Robert Toth

Left side: Yagi Meitatsu performing movements from Sanchin, Tensho, and Kururunfa katas. Right side: Yagi Meitoku in classic Goju-ryu movement.

All photos courtesy of Robert Toth.

Introduction

A famous man once said, "If you never forget where you come from, you can see more clearly where you're going." Lineage is the credentials that many people use in their search for a good karate instructor. Who did the teacher train with and who did his teacher train with? If possible, the history will be traced back to the absolute beginning. The need to track down the most direct descendent of the originator of a style is a result of the student wanting to learn whatever secrets the originator possessed. If the lineage is direct, it is more probable the secrets of the style will be passed on.

Yagi Meitatsu's lineage is very clear. His father was his only karate teacher. The elder Yagi was also a senior student of Goju-ryu karate founder Miyagi Chojun.

Background of Goju-ryu and Yagi Meitatsu

Miyagi Chojun was born on April 25, 1888 in Naha, Okinawa. The Miyagi family was wealthy as a result of importing medicinal products from China. When Miyagi was five years old, the successor to the main family passed away. As was the custom, Miyagi was adopted as the heir. Miyagi's mother was convinced that her son had to be both mentally and physically strong to face the world as the head of a family. When Miyagi was eleven years old, his mother arranged for him to start martial arts training with Arakaki Ryuko (1875-1961) of Naha (Sells, 2000: 81). Arakaki then introduced Miyagi to Higashionna Kanryo when Miyagi was fourteen years old (Higaonna, 1985: 25).

Higashonna had established a style of martial arts which was later called Naha-te, a combination of Chinese gongfu and Okinawan techniques (Porta and McCabe, 1994: 64). He had become interested in the martial arts when he was fourteen or fifteen years old. He first trained with Arakaki Seisho, one of the king's warriors. When the Ryukyu Government sent Arakaki to China, he recommended that the young Kanryo study with Kojo Taitai of Kumemura village. After two years, Higashionna arranged passage on a ship to Fujian Province, China, to continue his martial arts training. In Fujian, Higashonna became a student of Ko Ryuru (Sells, 2000: 45, 47). *Ryuru*, which means "to proceed," was a nickname. *Ko* is a suffix that means "big brother" (McCarthy, 1995: 38). It is not known how long Higashonna stayed in China. But on his return to Okinawa, his fame spread and he taught the martial arts in his courtyard.

Miyagi Chojun trained with his teacher until Higashionna's death in 1915. After this, Miyagi made at least two trips to China to further his knowledge of the martial arts. He then set about perfecting the Naha-te he had inherited from Higashionna Kanryo (Sells, 2000: 45, 47, 82).

In 1929, Miyagi Chojun sent his senior student, Shinzato Jinan, to a meeting of various martial artists in Kyoto, Japan. When Shinzato was asked the name of his style, he replied *Hanko-ryu* (half-hard style) rather than admit that the style didn't have a name. After returning to Okinawa, he mentioned the story to his teacher. Miyagi decided a better name would be Goju-ryu. He borrowed the name from a poem in the *Bubishi*, an ancient Chinese martial arts book. The poem explains eight martial arts concepts. One is the idea of hardness and softness (Alexander, 1998: 53, 54). The line in the *Bubishi* reads: "The way of inhaling and exhaling is both hardness and softness" (Yagi, Wheeler and Vickerson, 1998: 65). Miyagi thought it was important to name his art for the future (Yagi, 2004, e-mail).

Although Miyagi called his style Goju-ryu, he never had a sign with the name written on it at his school. In 1933, Miyagi Chojun's art was formally registered as "Goju-ryu" with the Association for the Martial Virtues of Great Japan (*Dai Nippon Butokukai*) (Higaonna, 1985: 28).

Yagi Meitatsu's father, Yagi Meitoku, was born on March 6, 1912 in Naha, Okinawa (Yagi, Wheeler, and Vickerson, 1998: 50). His grandfather took him to Miyagi Chojun when he was thirteen years old. Yagi explained to Miyagi that Meitoku's ancestor, Jana Teido, had been a great man in politics and a great martial artist as well. He hoped that in the future Meitoku would also become a great martial artist (Yagi, e-mail 2004).

Yagi Meitoku in 1960. Note the bandage on the right hand over his knuckles. The story is that after many years of training with a punching post (*makiwara*), he carved the callouses off his knuckles with a knife and started over again.

Miyagi Chojun was very disciplined and strict. One time a student came to the training hall whistling; Miyagi told him not to return. Another wore a towel around his neck and was also told not to come back (Yagi, 2004, interview). There were only two or three other students training at the time. Later, there would be four or five. During his classes, Miyagi would teach warm-ups, basics, and forms (*kata*) (Yagi, Wheeler, and Vickerson, 1998: 56, 57).

Many people came to train with Miyagi. He worked them very hard and many students left. If they stayed, Miyagi would teach them the basic Sanchin kata. This would go on for two or three years. It was hard training. Miyagi would leave black and blue marks on his students from checking their stances in Sanchin. The demanding training weeded out all but the most dedicated.

Originally, Miyagi taught only four katas: Sanchin, Seisan, Seiunchin, and Tensho. But later, he taught Yagi Meitoku all the Goju-ryu forms. Yagi, who was only in high school at the time, was the first of Miyagi's students to learn the complete Goju-ryu system (Babladelis, 1992: 41, 42). This was pre-World War II.

The Second World War was a devastating time for Okinawa and its people. In 1942, the Imperial Japanese forces swept through Southeast Asia. The Japanese felt they were driving the wicked Europeans and Americans out. But by 1943, the tide had decisively turned. Allied forces were pouring into the Pacific and Japan was in retreat. Okinawa formed an outer defense line for mainland Japan and lay in the Allies' path. Naha came under attack for the first time in October 1944. Ninety percent of the city was burned. The city of Shuri was bombed again and again. Okinawan civil defense measures were hopelessly inadequate. Tokyo gave little thought to Okinawa and did virtually nothing to prepare it for invasion. By the end of the Battle for Okinawa it is estimated that 62,489 civilians perished. One in eight of the civilian population was dead. No family remained untouched (Kerr, 2000: 463, 465-467, 472).

Miyagi Chojun suffered personal tragedy with the deaths of two of his daughters and a son (Toguchi, 2001: 20). As well, Shinzato Jinan, Miyagi's senior student, was killed during the early fighting of the Battle of Okinawa in 1945. There was no karate training during the war. Afterwards, Miyagi taught outside in his yard.

Left: Yagi Meitoku in his garden dojo.
Right: Meitoku during a demonstration at the Shuri Castle in 1992.

On October 8, 1953, at the age of sixty-five, Miyagi Chojun suddenly died (Porta and McCabe, 1994: 69). The Miyagi family held a meeting to decide which of his students their father would have wanted to carry on his system. They awarded Miyagi's belt and uniform to Yagi Meitoku, who was one of his first students (Babladelis, 1992: 40).

Yagi named his school "Meibukan" or "house of the pure warrior" to distinguish it from the schools that were opened by other students of Miyagi Chojun (Yagi, Wheeler, and Vickerson, 1998: 49).

Yagi's oldest son, Meitatsu, was born in Kume, Naha City, Okinawa, Japan on July 7, 1944. At the age of five, Meitatsu started karate training with his father. They trained in their backyard six days a week for two hours a day (Yagi, interview 2004). Yagi Meitatsu has never read a book about karate or watched a karate video. All of his knowledge about Goju-ryu karate comes from his father and master (Trebilcock, 2004).

Yagi Meitatsu attended university and worked in the United States from 1964 to 1970. He has also worked in Guam, Saipan, and the Philippines.

Yagi Meitoku chose his eldest son to be the first to learn all facets of Meibukan Goju-ryu. Yagi Meitoku gave Meitatsu the title of *hanshi* (IMGKA, 2004) or a respected master and 10th-degree black belt (Farkis and Corcoran, 1983: 103, 129). This is the only time Yagi Meitoku gave this title.

On February 7, 2003, Yagi Meitoku died at the age of 92 (IMGKA, 2004). Just five months before his death he gave a demonstration at the Budokan in Naha (Trebilcock, 2004).

Yagi Meitatsu as a
sixteen-year-old black belt.

Yagi Meitatsu carries on the teaching and traditions of his father. Now at the age of sixty, Mr. Yagi has retired from his profession and devotes all of his time to propagating Goju-ryu karate all over the world. He has said, "This is my responsibility. This is my life."

The Yagi family crest was created by Yagi Meitoku. Side by side are the characters for "sun and moon." The sun is bigger than the moon. As the sun and moon traverse the sky, so one must complete the study of each technique. The horizontal line in the "sun" character on the left is thick, while to two for "moon" are thin to symbolize the outside and the inside of the body. The character on the left has no exit, but the one on the right does. This stands for inhaling and exhaling.

INTERVIEW WITH YAGI MEITATSU

Movements from the katas Seisan (left) and Seipai (right).

▸ Could you explain the theory of Goju-ryu karate?

Go means hard and *ju* means soft. Physically, both hard and soft techniques are used. Mentally, it is to be soft to other people and hard on yourself. *Go* or hard is Sanchin kata and *ju* or soft is Tensho. Sanchin is practiced to create a strong body and to develop internal energy (*ki*) techniques. Tensho is the closing kata. I was told that Tensho was made by the founder of Goju-ryu, Miyagi Chojun. It comes from the Chinese kenpo exercise called *rokkishu*.[1] Sanchin and Tensho have to do with breath control. Sanchin is mostly closed hand and Tensho is mostly open hand.

Philosophically, when you achieve something for yourself, when you've learned something, you have to share it with others. This is inhale and exhale—*go ju*. But I must explain that in my day, we were not supposed to ask questions like this. We just waited until the teacher told us.

▸ Let me understand this. One of your goals is to spread Goju-ryu karate, the way your father taught it, all over the world. But part of that traditional karate training is that the student shouldn't ask questions?

Yes (laughs). Sometimes I see white belts or green belts asking, "What does this mean?" "What does that mean?" But I know it's too early for them. Sometimes I'll explain and sometimes I won't.

To take an educational view, when a child is in elementary school and has a homework assignment and the parent does it for him. The child may get 100%, but he didn't learn anything. First let him try. He must labor by himself. If he cannot do it, then you try to help.

I watched my father for fifty years. I waited until he explained or until I could figure it out for myself without being told.

▸ Do you think that's what the student should do today? Watch you for fifty years?

Yes. That is my desire (laughs).

▸ The idea of doing an article in a magazine would be totally foreign to your father or to Miyagi Chojun. They'd never consider it. But in North America, the karate student wants to buy a magazine so they can see pictures of the master and learn some secret about the martial art they're training in. It's rather different. Don't you think?

Many people asked my father to write a karate book. You know what he said?—"My teacher, Miyagi Chojun, didn't write a book so, how can I?"

When somebody studies from a karate book or a video, it's different. You must study physically. If you have videos and books, there's no need to practice. But without videos and books, you automatically practice at least twice a week so as not to forget.

To perfect a kata, it has to be practiced 10,000 times. So if a kata is practiced once a day for a year, it will take thirty years to perfect it.

Some schools have one whole wall of mirrors. But a mirror will not correct your kata. It can only be corrected by the teacher.

1-4) Mr. Yagi Meitatsu demonstrating several of
the conventional techniques as taught by Miyagi Chojun.

In the old days, there was only a small hand mirror in the dojo. My father told me the reason. He said that when you come into the school, you have a mild face before you start. After you've practiced for two hours, you have a hard face. So, when you finish class and are ready to go home, you look in the small mirror until you return to a mild face.

When I tell a story at a seminar, how it is understood depends on how far each person is into their training. Maybe the white belt will understand 30% of the story, a green belt 50%, a brown belt 75%, and a black belt 100%. But some students will understand 120%. They can read between the lines. They can see what I'm trying to say behind the story. This is important. My point is 100% is not enough. There is no short cut. My father, my teacher, didn't teach secret techniques. I had to achieve them myself (laughs).

▶ SECRET TECHNIQUES?

Sometimes in the movies they show secret techniques being written onto a scroll and kept locked in a room. The ninja breaks in, steals the scroll, and studies it. That is not secret techniques. Secret techniques are open to the public but nobody can imitate. Like Bruce Lee, Jet Li, and Jackie Chan. They show everything but other people cannot imitate them. Open to everyone but nobody can imitate. This is the secret technique.

Techniques are different for each person because they depend on physical structure. When my father taught techniques, I could not imitate him 100% because there was different physical ability and we had a different way of practicing. I watched him for fifty years but couldn't do what he did. We had different body structures. Secret techniques depend on the person. You have to be close to the teacher as often as you can because he can't show them in a short time.

▶ HOW DO YOU THINK KARATE HAS CHANGED IN OKINAWA?

When I was small, we didn't show other people our martial art. We had a high fence around our yard. When we practiced, people would come and try to watch. That was the old days. Today, it's open to everyone.

Even five or ten years ago, I would only teach Meibukan members. Now I have a rounded corner. (Mr. Yagi made as if to cut the corner off of the table we were sitting at with his finger.) I will teach anyone if they are willing to study.

Another change occurred when Okinawa was returned to Japan in 1975.[2] That was the time sport karate or competition karate started in Okinawa. The [All] Japan Karate Association wanted Okinawa to take part in their domestic competitions. A delegation came to discuss the direction the competition would take. We agreed that the free sparring should follow their rules because they started that. But the kata had to be as we did them. But the Japan Karate

Association decided that everyone, including Okinawa, had to follow the Japanese standards. Each traditional kata has its own characteristics. But the JKA changed them to make it easy to score for tournaments. And for tournaments they don't practice the katas in the correct order. There is no time for them to study the basic katas of *Gekisai Itchi*, *Gekisai Ni* or *Sanchin*. They skip them. They only know how to win at a tournament.

But we have no intention to argue with the Japan Karate Association. We don't say that they are bad and we are good. It is just different.[3]

Left, application of a technique from Shishochin kata; right, from Sempai kata.

▸ COULD YOU TELL US THE DIFFERENCE BETWEEN TRADITIONAL KARATE AND SPORT KARATE?

The difference between sport karate and traditional karate is sport karate is age-limited. When you are young, you can do sport karate; but traditional karate can be done up until your last breath. Most of the sport karate in Japan is done by university students. But when they leave school and go to work, they stop competing because you cannot go to the company with a bruised eye or broken teeth. Sport karate teaches mostly physical techniques and how to win. Traditional karate teaches how not to lose.

But sport karate is not real fighting. Even the Kyokushin[4] style is not real fighting because they are not supposed to attack the weak points of the body like the eyes. In an actual fight, the opponent will kill you like in a war. So, traditional karate teaches to attack the opponent's weak points.

It's the same with judo and jujutsu. Jujutsu had many very good techniques. But they were fatal techniques. So, Kano Jigoro, the founder of judo, took all the dangerous techniques out and made it safer. Even ladies can compete in judo.

That's why the Gracies are so strong. They kept the traditional ways. In Brazil in the old days, a Japanese jujutsu man taught the Gracie grandfather. He passed it on to his sons and grandsons. Now nobody can win against them. Even the Japanese cannot win because the Gracies know the old techniques.[5]

In the old days, there were many dangerous techniques in karate, as well. I've shown you some. This is real traditional karate. When you make a fist, it's short and dull. If you open the hand, it's long and sharp.

We try to spread traditional karate as we have studied with Master Yagi Meitoku. Our main purpose is not to produce many champions but to produce a fine person. Our teacher always said that, when you study karate, don't put your main purpose to study technique itself, but to study the way of life through karate. Everybody has twenty-four hours in a day. Karate training is only two hours a day. The mental part is the other twenty-two hours. You have to train the spiritual first in order to be a good karate man. Spiritual and physical training have to develop together. We are not perfect. Everybody has good and bad points. It's important to train your heart first.

Yagi Meitatsu demonstrating techniques.

People are coming back to traditional karate to study history, applications of movement in katas, and details in technique. Today with the internet and everything, people are learning about Goju-ryu karate and the successor of the style. People from many countries are contacting us for training. At the moment, there are Meibukan Goju-ryu schools in the USA, Canada, England, Italy, Australia, Israel, India, Bermuda, Sri Lanka, and the Philippines.

Yagi Meitatsu correcting a technique found in Sempai kata.

▶ THANK YOU MR. YAGI. I REALLY APPRECIATE HOW MUCH YOU'VE HELPED ME BY ALLOWING ME TO TRAIN WITH YOU.

It's my pleasure.

Conclusion

Martial arts training is like having a puzzle face down on your dining room table. Every time you train, you get to turn one of the pieces over. In time, some of the pieces fit together and the student is able to see what appears to be a picture. Over many years of training, more of the puzzle pieces fit and the picture becomes larger and more detailed.

Sometimes, the student thinks they've found the perfect piece, the one that will make the picture almost complete. But it doesn't turn out that way because our understanding of what the pieces are changes. The martial arts are a puzzle that must be worked on for a lifetime.

Notes

[1] *Rokkishu* or "the six wind hands" refers to six types of spearhand or penetration techniques used in gongfu (Alexander, 1992: 52).

[2] The American occupation of Okinawa ended on May 15, 1972, having lasted for twenty-seven years. Okinawa regarded the reversion to Japan as the cure for all the real or imagined ills and evils reportedly caused by the Americans (Kerr, 2000: 554).

[3] The All-Okinawa Karate Federation (AOKF) resisted because many of its members felt that Okinawa, the birthplace of karate, would be dominated by Japanese interests. A split occurred within the AOKF, pitting those who felt that Okinawa should take part in what some saw as the future of karate, against those who pressed for independence and a resurgence of pride in things Okinawan (Sells, 2000: 200).

[4] Kyokushinkai is a karate style founded by Korean-born Oyama Masutatsu. It was influenced by circular Chinese techniques and the powerful karate of Funakoshi Gichin and Goju-ryu karate. Kyokushinkai advocates body contact to help students overcome fear (Corcoran, Farkas, and Sobel, 1993: 67).

[5] In 1914, Maeda Esai, also known as Count Koma, came to Brazil. He was a former world champion of jujutsu. He became a friend of Gastao Gracie. As a show of friendship, Maeda taught the son of Gastao, Carlos Gracie, jujutsu. In 1925, Carlos and his four brothers opened the first jujutsu academy in Brazil (Gracie, video 1988).

Bibliography

Alexander, G., and Penland, K. (1999). *Bubishi: Martial arts spirit*. Second edition. Reliance, TN: Yamazato Publications.

Alexander, G. (1998). *Okinawa: Island of karate*. Reliance, TN: Yamazato International.

Babladelis, P. (1992, December). The sensei who received Chojun Miyagi's belt. *Black Belt*, 40-44.

Corcoran, J., Farkas, E., and Sobel S. (1993). *The original martial arts encyclopedia*. Los Angeles: Pro-Action Publishing.

Farkas, E., and Corcoran, J. (1983). *The Overlook martial arts dictionary*. Woodstock, NY: The Overlook Press.

Gracie Jiu-jitsu in Action, video, (1988). Torrance, CA: Brajitsu.

Higaonna, M. (1985). *Traditional karate do Okinawa Goju-ryu, Volume 1*. Tokyo: Minato.

IMGKA (2004). International Meibukan Gojyu-ryu Karate Association website www.imgka.com.

Kerr, G. (2000). *Okinawa: The history of an island people*. Revised edition. Boston: Tuttle Publishing.

McCarthy, P. (1995). *The bible of karate: Bubishi*. Boston: Tuttle Publishing.

Porta, J., and McCabe, J. (1994). The karate of Chojun Miyagi. *Journal of Asian Martial Arts*, 3(3), 63-70.

Sells, J. (2000). *Unante: The secrets of karate*. Hollywood: W.M. Hawley.

Toguchi, S. (2001). *Okinawan Goju-ryu II*. Santo Clarita, CA: Ohara Publications.

Trebilcock, K. (2004, May 14). Interview in St. Catharines, Ontario, Canada.

Yagi, M. (2004, April 16). E-mail communication.

Yagi, M. (2004, May 14). Interview held in St. Catharines, Ontario, Canada.

Yagi, M., Wheeler, C., and Vickerson, B. (1998). *Okinawa karate-do Goju-ryu Meibukan*. Dundas, Ontario, Canada: Action.

Acknowledgment

The author would like to thank Mr. Yagi Meitatsu for providing pictures of his father for this chapter. Also, thank you to Carl Wheeler and Ken Trebilcock for appearing in the photos and their help with the chapter.

chapter 2

Steve Arneil and the British Kyokushinkai: An Interview

by Graham Noble

Mas Oyama and Steve Arneil.
Oyama at left instructing at his dojo in Japan. Steve Arneil is second
from the left (facing the camera) among the group of students in paired practice.
All photos courtesy of Graham Noble except where noted.

Introduction

This interview with Steve Arneil (8th-dan) was conducted on the eve of the 21st British Kyokushinkai Championships at Crystal Palace, London. Although this occurred in 1996, publishing this interview in the *Journal of Asian Martial Arts* now makes it available to all interested in learning about a man who is, and has been, a very important figure both in British, and Kyokushinkai Karate history. As well as being the leading figure in British Kyokushinkai since 1965, he was the coach of the British Karate Team in a golden era which saw it win the World Championship and become a major force in tournament karate.

His life has been "a life in Kyokushin." He started training at the famous Oyama Dojo when the style itself was only a few years old, lived through its development into a real power in the karate world, and saw at first hand the problems which later set in. These problems led eventually to his break with the headquarters, but his emotional links with Oyama Masutatsu [Mas], and his roots in Kyokushinkai continue to run deep. After the interview, when we talked about the passing of Mas Oyama, and the circumstances which followed, he was close to tears several times.

I really enjoyed my short time with Steve Arneil and his group. The tournament, which I attended, has a deserved reputation for hard fighting, respect, and sportsmanship. My thanks to Liam Keaveney for his hospitality and help in arranging the interview; to Pete Rippin for making the initial contacts and for ferrying me about; and to Steve Arneil himself, for his friendliness, honesty, and straightforwardness.

MEETING MAS OYAMA

Mas Oyama.
Photo courtesy of the International Karate Organization.

▸ STEVE, WHEN YOU FIRST ARRIVED IN JAPAN IN LATE 1960, DID YOU GO THERE SPECIFICALLY TO LEARN KARATE?

Hmmm, not really. Coming to Kyokushinkai seemed one of those things in your life which is fated. I never planned it. Actually I had trained before in Africa in Shorin Kempo with a Chinese teacher. I liked that very much. At that time I was also involved in judo, and I liked boxing, but because of the problems in boxing, I concentrated on judo, then kempo.

This was in Northern Rhodesia. I also used to travel down to South Africa. At that time, there was rather a lot of emigration from Japan to Brazil, and when they stopped over in South Africa, we'd meet them and if any had martial arts experience we'd take them to the dojos in Durban. So I was learning karate from this one, from that one, from all kinds of people. I just wanted to learn, and I seemed to be very much attracted to the Eastern forms.

Finally, I decided I wanted to go to the East. My ambition was to go to China, and I did go there and studied in China for a while but we had problems there and had to get out. So I went back to Kowloon, but I wasn't too happy with the teaching there. It wasn't what I'd had in the beginning. Then I was told that I would be suited to a strong form of karate taught by a man called Mas Oyama in Japan.

▸ SO HE WAS WELL KNOWN EVEN THEN?

He was heard of. So then I worked my way to Japan and arrived in Yokohama. I didn't speak any Japanese. The only Japanese I knew was "Kodokan" [the headquarters of judo], so I went there and did some judo, and that is where I met my friend, Bob Bolton. I also met Donn Draeger, a great budoman, and we became friends.

I tried some karate dojos. I went to the Shotokan dojo, the JKA, which was just below the Kodokan, and I met people like Kase and so on. It was great, and they were very nice, but—It's difficult to explain, but it wasn't my cup of tea.

I also trained with Yamaguchi, "The Cat." I didn't know it at that time but Yamaguchi had been closely linked to Mr. Oyama. And I thought it was quite good. I liked it.

▸ WHAT WAS GOGEN YAMAGUCHI LIKE? DID HE ACTUALLY TEACH AT THE DOJO?

Oh, a very nice man. When I knew him, he was an excellent karate man. And yes, he taught the classes.

▸ WAS THE KUMITE HARD?

In those years, yes. With both Yamaguchi and Kyokushin, it was budo. It wasn't classified as a sport. And so the dojo fighting was fairly realistic. The object was to develop high level character, as well as how to fight, how to protect yourself.

Anyway, I spoke to Donn, and he said he knew Mr. Oyama! So he took me up to the first dojo of Kyokushin. That was behind Rikkyo University. When I arrived there—it was just a small place, but you could feel the atmosphere. Donn introduced me to my first contact with Kyokushin, Mr. Kurosaki, a brilliant karate man.

▶ COULD YOU TELL US SOMETHING ABOUT KUROSAKI KENJI. HE WAS KNOWN FOR HIS STRONG SPIRIT, WASN'T HE?

Oh, tremendously strong spirit! He never asked from anybody anything unless he did it himself. He was that type of man. And he was a tremendous motivator, very disciplined, a fine character. Donn introduced me to him and then I sat down to watch the training.

After the training had finished, Donn said to Mr. Kurosaki that I wanted to meet Mr. Oyama and train in Kyokushin. Mr. Kurosaki replied saying that Mr. Oyama wasn't there—he was away teaching in America. But if I wanted, I could come and watch. To me, this was a bit of a shock, as I'd traveled all this way looking for this, and now I was told I could just sit and watch. The other clubs wanted me to join straight-away. I thought it was strange.

Donn F. Draeger.
Photo courtesy of Robert W. Smith.

Mas Oyama's dojo.
He is standing in the back, far right.
Steve Arneil kneels in the front row, second from the left.

▸ WHAT STRUCK YOU ABOUT THE KYOKUSHINKAI DOJO? WHY DID YOU FEEL IT WAS DIFFERENT FROM THE OTHERS?

Discipline. Discipline on a very high level, and respect. And friendliness. They would talk to me. I felt they weren't trying to impress me. They were just strong karate practitioners.

Anyway, I said OK. But Donn said, "You have to come every day to watch." I asked when Mr. Oyama was coming back, but they said they didn't know. So I continued to watch, and what I saw I liked. The training was strong. It had rhythm, it was "punch-punch-punch." The teacher was never quite satisfied. Then the fighting started, and I was impressed by that. I wondered why they didn't get hurt, but their bodies were conditioned. And never, ever, did they abuse their position. They knew how far to take it.

▸ WE SOMETIMES HEAR STORIES ABOUT BULLYING IN JAPANESE DOJOS.

I have heard stories like this, but I can put my hand on my heart and say that I never saw that in the Kyokushinkai dojo of that time. I was treated absolutely fairly as a *kohai* [junior student]. It didn't matter about color or religion or anything. I was a *kohai*, and I had to do my duties as a kohai. I was treated exactly the same as everyone else. Nobody ever tried to take advantage. What the Japanese white belt got, I got. I've heard stories later on which sadden me, but when I was in Japan everyone was treated fairly.

▸ SO HOW LONG DID YOU SIT WATCHING THE CLASSES?

About a month. I went up there regularly and sat and watched. Then finally this man walked through the door and I knew immediately it was him. It was just his aura, his personality.

And then Donn Draeger was called because Mas Oyama didn't speak English very much. Donn explained my situation and Mr. Oyama said, "Fine, but you know, if you train with me, you train for life. Think about it. A lot of things can go wrong in life, but you must train in what I teach you." And I said, "Yes, I'll take it on." Then he said, "You start as a kohai, and you must train regularly. If you stop training, we'll kick you out." I said I understood, then he said that as a mark of appreciation, he would give me my first karate gi. And that's where it started.

As a kohai, I had to go in and clean the dojo. It was an old dojo, but man it was spotless. The *sempai* [senior students] would just put their gis on the floor and the kohais would pick them up and it was their responsibility to wash and iron the gis and hang them up on a peg the next day. And if all the gis weren't well cleaned all the kohais would get it in the neck.

And then there was cleaning the toilets out. The first time I had to clean the toilets out, I got the shock of my life. You know Ashihara, the founder of Ashihara Karate? We were kohais together in the dojo. We had to go and clean the toilets, and they weren't flush ones. The toilet then was just a big bucket, and we had to take these buckets out, walk down the road, and throw them in a special area where the truck would come and take it away. And then we had to wash the buckets out with our hands before we put them back. Even to this day, I still shudder when I think about it [laughing].

But then as time went on we trained hard! It was hard training. But it was beneficial training, because we didn't do anything without a reason. It was said to me, and I say this today to my students—"I can teach you, I can help you, but there are two things I can't do: think for you and do it for you. That's your job, and if you can't do it, get out of the dojo."

▶ COULD YOU TELL US A LITTLE MORE ABOUT MAS OYAMA. FOR EXAMPLE, HOW BIG WAS HE—FIVE FOOT SEVEN, FIVE FOOT EIGHT?

Yes, around that. He was a little bigger than me. But at that time he was just a very powerfully built man. He really was.

▶ HE DID QUITE A BIT OF WEIGHT TRAINING AT ONE TIME?

He did weight training to supplement his karate, by himself. You know, we'd be doing our punching training, and he'd be lying at the back of the dojo pushing a weight "Uss! Uss! Uss!," while we'd be punching.

▶ HE'D BE BENCH PRESSING WHILE SHOUTING THE COMMANDS FOR PUNCHING?

Yes, while shouting and encouraging us to train harder. That's the way training was with him. Then he'd do squats, and so on.

▶ WHAT KIND OF WEIGHTS DID HE USE? HEAVY? LIGHT?

The weights were fairly heavy. He always said that the body itself is very strong, but you should train with weights which supplement your training. You know, he wasn't talking about being a muscle man, posing, or getting cut up. He built his body for power in karate.

▶ I SPOKE TO BOBBY LOWE ON THE PHONE ONCE AND HE TOLD ME THAT HE'D SEEN MAS OYAMA BEND A COIN.

I have seen Oyama bend a Japanese coin with his fingers, although I can't vouch for the strength of Japanese coins then. ...Still a terrific feat.

▶ BOBBY LOWE ALSO TOLD ME THAT MAS OYAMA WAS THE STRONGEST MAN HE HAD EVER MET, NOT ONLY PHYSICALLY BUT MENTALLY.

There's no doubt that Mas Oyama was a very powerful man, physically and mentally, but I wouldn't say he was the only man in the world with these qualities. I also met some people in China who impressed me tremendously with their willpower and their strength, and I've seen others in my travels. But yes, I would say Oyama was one of the exceptional people.

▶ I'VE BEEN TOLD THAT AROUND THE LATE 1950S, EARLY 1960S, MAS OYAMA CHALLENGED ALL THE OTHER SCHOOLS TO TAKE PART IN A NATIONAL CONTEST TO DECIDE WHICH WAS THE STRONGEST STYLE. DO YOU KNOW ANYTHING ABOUT THAT?

I've heard of that, but I wasn't aware of any challenge when I was in Japan. The only time when we were part of a challenge, that I know of, was when we were challenged by the Thai boxers. That took place when I was in Japan.

▶ SO TO YOUR KNOWLEDGE, HE NEVER BADMOUTHED THE OTHER KARATE STYLES?

No, he never badmouthed any style. All he said was, "We are the best!" He said that "We are budo," and even at that time, the art was changing into a sport. He said that in time to come, a sports-only karate man would find it difficult to deal with a street situation. And his prediction came true. A boy may be excellent at the sport, but not able to deliver in a street situation. Although of course it will help them to some degree.

TRAINING AT THE KYOSHINKAI

▶ COULD YOU TAKE US THROUGH A TRAINING SESSION AT THE KYOKUSHINKAI DOJO AT THAT TIME?

OK, I'll take you through an evening session when I was there. Firstly, you had to be there at 7:30. At 7:15, the drums began to beat, and you could hear those drums quite a distance away. When that drum stopped, you didn't bother going into the dojo late, because you just weren't going to train. No excuses.

You began the training by going through the procedures of bowing, meditation, and loosening up and stretching exercises—and the stretching in those days was hard! They would pull your legs apart to work on the splits and I had a hard time with that. I used to play rugby and my legs were quite stiff at that time, but they did get my legs apart! Then you did a lot of physical training like push-ups, and a lot of breathing exercises, because he was very strict on breathing. He said that if a person doesn't breathe, he's dead. So we did a lot of rapid breathing [*nogare*] and a lot of sonorous, abdominal breathing [*ibuki*].

Then we would do our classical warm-up. We would go into *sanchin* stance, he would stand in the front, then we would go through the various techniques —fore-fist thrust, back-fist strike, knife hand strike—it would average about seventeen techniques.

Steve Arneil playing the attacker in the knife-defense section of Oyama's book, *What is Karate* (1963). *Photo courtesy of the publisher.*

More knife-defense technique from *What is Karate* (1963).
Photo courtesy of the publisher.

▶ How many repetitions did you do of each?

Oh Christ—he would start with a count of ten from the highest grade, then the next highest ten, then the next ten, ten, ten—and it would go up to how many black belts there were.

▶ So Oyama himself would do all this with you?

Oh yes, he trained every time.

Mas Oyama.
Photo courtesy of the International Karate Organization.

▶ That must have impressed you.

Of course. This is what I liked about him. He did it with us. This is why to this day, I will do my damnedest to train as much as my students as possible. Following on from the hand techniques we would then do the kicks the same way. Then when that was finished, we would go through *kihon*, the basics, moving through the techniques in forward stance, horse stance, back stance, middle section thrust, upper section thrust, blocks, combinations. He was very, very strict on basics. He wanted the forward stance right, he wanted the back stance, right. Actually he was a bit of a perfectionist and it was very difficult to please him. And until he was happy with it he wouldn't move on to the next technique.

Then we would do free-sparring and that was when you put the little bandages on your fists. That was when the kohais like myself got a little apprehensive. All the black belts would line up, then you had to get up and start from the top of the line, working your way to the bottom. Each black belt had his own ways, and some were heavier handed than others, but they were fair. There were never really any injuries because we were all fairly well trained. The only thing was, we used to hit to the face.

▶ This was with the hands wrapped?

All we used to do was take some bandages and wrap them round the knuckles so that we wouldn't cut the skin. And you really had to learn to block. If you didn't block, you got smacked. The only thing we weren't allowed to do at that time, was kick to the groin. And we weren't kicking to the legs when I was there. Kicking to the legs only came in after the boys came back from Thailand. Otherwise, it was anything goes.

▶ How long did the free-style sparring [jyu-kumite] last?

Well, there was no set time. The thing was, at that dojo you started at 7:30, and if he fancied it, you would go on to 12:00. Or if he wanted a short session, you'd finish at 10:00. When you went to the dojo, you went to train and there was no time schedule. If the training ran late, it was your problem how you got home. These were the things you had to accept.

▶ Did you do any prearranged forms before the free-sparring?

Not really. Before free-sparring, we'd do the combinations—moving forward, moving back, front kicks, round kicks, spinning back kicks. We didn't do the things that you saw in Shotokan, for example, the prearranged techniques.

▶ So you didn't do three-step kumite for example?

Mas Oyama believed you learned to fight by fighting. Three-step wasn't going to help you with that. For form, you did kata, and believe it or not Mas Oyama stressed kata a lot. He said your kata was there to train you to think. Teaching three-step kumite isn't going to help you in the street. When you did free-sparring, you'd bow, then the guy would throw anything at you he could and you'd have to block it. You didn't say "he's going to throw a roundhouse kick and I'm going to step to the side and then do this or that." He didn't really go for that because he said it was based on a misconception. On the street, no-one would let you know, "OK, I'm coming in with a big round kick."

▶ So he thought that type of training was too stiff, not natural?

Yes, our fighting was very strong, very disciplined, very accurate, but we weren't like Shotokan, Shukokai, Wado-ryu—you know, block, "bang" counter and then step out—which of course was very good, and I still say is an excellent exercise for karate practitioners. I do it myself now with my students because I think it has a place in a karate practitioner's overall development.

▸ Do you think this Kyokushinkai style of fighting came out of Mas Oyama's own experience? He said he had fought boxers, wrestlers and so on, when he was in America for example.

I think so, because you know he had to get in the ring and fight under any rules.

▸ Did he spar at the dojo with you?

Oh yes, but very seldom. I am one of the very few people privileged to have sparred with him quite a few times; me and a few other black belts.

▸ What was he like to spar with?

Phenomenal. You just couldn't hit him. If you kicked him, his hand was there, if you punched to his face, his arm was there. If you moved this way, he was out of the way, if you moved that way, he was in on you. I'm talking of his heyday, when I was around.

I've got a film, which I'm very privileged to have, of me actually fighting him. It was taken in Jordan when I was private tutor to the Royal Family and he came out to see us.

▸ What techniques did he use in free-sparring?

At that time, when I was doing free-sparring with him, he didn't really have the flexibility in his legs that he used to have with the round kicks, but his hands were absolutely brilliant. You know, we'd do the circular blocking movement, and it was like a windmill. Your hand is like a windmill, or a fan. When a fan is going slowly, you can put your finger in and out, but when the fan speeds up, you can't put your finger in. So your reactions and hand speed work in that manner, and that made him almost untouchable.

▸ Was he quick as well, because you sometime wonder whether a person with a powerful build like that might lose something in speed?

He was very fast. He was muscular, but he built his body up for the purpose of doing what he wanted to do in karate. He didn't build himself up to pose. His body was big, strong, but it was ready to move like lightning, and powerful enough to do any type of block or defense.

▸ Could you tell us about some of the people who were at the dojo then. Kurosaki you've already mentioned.

Kurosaki was my favorite motivator for fighting. He had the gift of pushing you to the limit, and then he would ask for more.

▸ But he would do it himself?

He would be with you, yes. At that time, he was in charge of keeping the high level of fighting up.

▸ He must have been with the Kyokushin from the very start.

Yes, he was one of the first. Of course, if you were to go back in history, most of the original Kyokushin men came from other styles.

▸ I've heard that, like Oyama, he was with Yamaguchi of Goju and they started Kyokushin at the same time.

I don't really know about that.

▸ What about Yasuda Eiji, who does the kata in *What is Karate* (1959)?

Yasuda Eiji was a good karate man. He was tall, slim…a different character from Kurosaki. Kurosaki would be pushing, pushing, but Yasuda was more easy going. But in kumite he was like a snake—he would strike so fast you wouldn't know what hit you. He was the type of person who never showed any emotion, so you never knew when he was going to hit you or kick you. He would just look at you, then "bang!" and that would be it. A wonderful gentleman.

Yasuda Eiji demonstrating Saiha Kata.
Ishibashi Masami teaching.

▶ Ishibashi Masami?

You don't hear much about him. He kept in the background, but he was a very important person. He was an absolute perfectionist, especially in kata. He really got me into kata, and pushed me in kata. For example, in Saiha Kata, he could put a coin on the floor and start the kata from there. He would do the kata so perfectly that he would finish back on that coin.

He also had a tremendous way of explaining kata in a practical way, not a mystical way. Very down to earth. How you did it, and why you did it that way.

And he also explained that many of the things in the kata may not represent what you see straight-away. In other words, sometimes a move is a link brought into the kata so that it flows, but it has no real fighting meaning. It has purpose in keeping the movement going.

▶ And it will adjust the shape and rhythm of the kata?

That's right. And you know, a lot of people try to create a meaning or application for every movement in the kata. Ishibashi would often say this is just a position, or a linking movement within the kata. Ishibashi was the one who was really in charge of kata at that time, along with Okada Hirofumi.

▶ Okada posed for most of the photographs in Oyama's *This is Karate* (1965).

Yes, he's in the old books. He was not only a brilliant fighter, but a brilliant kata man also.

Okada Hirofumi breaking to top off a bottle.
Photo from *This is Karate* (1965).

▶ WHAT GRADES DID THESE INSTRUCTORS HAVE AT THAT TIME?

In those days, I just knew them as "sensei," and a sensei at that time was a 3rd dan. When Mas Oyama came in, I called him sensei too.

▶ THEY DIDN'T PLACE A LOT OF EMPHASIS ON THE NUMBER OF DAN?

No. You were a sensei. As Oyama said in those years, it's not the grade that makes the person, it's the person that makes the grade. At that time I think Oyama was 6th dan, although I wouldn't put my life on it. I didn't really bother about that. All I knew was he was the Sensei. [Note: In his 1959 book, *What is Karate?*, Mas Oyama's grade is given as 8th dan]. Okada, Kurosaki, and Ishibashi were, I think, 3rd dan.

▶ THEY WOULD HAVE BEEN THE FIRST GENERATION OF KYOKUSHIN SENSEI?

Yes, they were the first generation of top sensei.

▶ AFTER THAT CAME THE GENERATION OF NAKAMURA TADASHI, SHIGERU OYAMA?

Nakamura Tadashi, Shigeru Oyama, and myself.

▶ AND HIDEYUKI ASHIHARA WAS AROUND THEN?

Ashihara was with me. We grew up in Kyokushin and got our grades together. We got our brown belts together. I failed my 1st dan test, but he passed. Then later I passed him and got my 2nd dan before him.

Left: Nakamura Tadashi.
Right: Akio Fujihira.

▸ Could you tell us about Nakamura?

Nakamura Tadashi was brilliant. He tended to take over, or take responsibility, along with Oyama Shigeru. If it had all worked out as it was meant to, and there were none of the difficulties that happened later. Nakamura Tadashi was groomed to be the next head of Kyokushin.

▸ He mentions that in his book, The Human Face of Karate.

Yes, he was groomed. We knew it, it was made quite clear, and we accepted he would be the next one to take over. It was intended that, as Mas Oyama got older, he would gradually take control. Shigeru Oyama would be following, and I was following in their footsteps. I was being groomed also—there was no restriction because I was a *gaijin* [non-Japanese]. I was a karate practitioner. I was a 2nd dan when Nakamura and Oyama were 3rd dans.

Then things started to develop. In 1965, I came to Europe and had a lot of hard work, because in those years you had Sensei Enoeda and Kanazawa and Suzuki here. Then I came along and, of course, in those years people thought that only a Japanese could teach karate.

▸ But Mas Oyama never believed that?

No. I begged him like hell, "Please send me a Japanese instructor!" He said, "If you're not good enough, you don't deserve to be there. I taught you to be a karate man. Teach you own students, let them learn among themselves." Which I did.

▸ His trust in you must have given you a lot of confidence.

Yes, because you know it was hard work. Let's face it, Enoeda, Kanazawa, Suzuki—they were fantastic instructors.

▸ To go back to Nakamura Tadashi, what was special about him?

Nakamura was a very powerful, but also a very deep thinking, karate practitioner. There was a lot of philosophy there, and even today with his own group, his philosophy is beautiful and deep. He was a brilliant karate man.

If I can put it this way—Nakamura Tadashi was a good strong karate man with a deep philosophy. He was good all round but his distinctive feature was this deepness. Shigeru was a fighter, and today his own organization will show you that: a fighting style. I was groomed to be in between these two in terms of character. Because I was fanatical on technique, I was also very prominent in kata, and I loved fighting. And even today, in my organization, I try to keep these qualities. I like the basics, the fighting, the kata, and I also like the respect and courtesy of karate as it should be.

The three of us were well matched. Nakamura Tadashi then went to America and did a wonderful job. Shigeru followed him, but before that, Bob Boulton, who was a 2nd dan, came back to Britain. I was going to leave Japan and Oyama asked if I would like to go to Europe to help Bob for a while, because he knew that eventually I wanted to go back to Africa. I said, OK I'll do that. So we came to Britain, but due to the problems in Africa at that time, and with my wife being Japanese, I then made the decision to stay in Europe.

▸ IF I CAN JUST ADD ONE MORE NAME FROM THOSE EARLY DAYS — JON BLUMING.

I knew Jon Bluming very well. He was a very robust, very strong fighting man. That's all he ever wanted to do.

Left: Oyama Shigeru (left) in a sword-catching demonstration with Nakamura Tadashi. Right: Jon Bluming (*photo courtesy of Jon Bluming*).

▸ Is it true that he had a standing $10,000 or, in some versions, $100,000 challenge to fight anyone?

I don't know about that.

▸ WAS HE TRAINING AT THE DOJO WHEN YOU WERE THERE?

No, Jon had just left. He had left the memory of ...

▸ A LEGEND?

Not a legend, but...a madman [laughing]! But, when I say "madman," I say in the best possible way, with a lot of respect. He was just so strong. He was like that at the Kodokan.

▶ HIS ABILITY IN BOTH JUDO AND KARATE MADE HIM A FORMIDABLE OPPONENT?

I would say Jon could have got into the Olympics in judo, but because of certain things, he wasn't chosen to represent Holland. I don't want to go into the politics, but I would say Bluming was better than Geesink. [Anton Geesink won the gold in judo at the 1964 Olympics held in Tokyo]. That's just my own opinion. But he was a brilliant judo man, and as a karate man, he was very good as well.

THE 100 MAN FIGHT

▶ CAN WE MOVE ON NOW TO YOUR 100-MAN FIGHT. YOU WERE THE FIRST PERSON TO COMPLETE THIS TEST?

So I believe.

▶ MAS OYAMA MUST HAVE HAD CONFIDENCE IN YOU TO PICK YOU FOR THAT.

I was surprised when he chose me, because people had tried before and been unsuccessful. When he spoke to me about it, I said, "You're crazy!" He said, "I think you can do it." I said, "I don't know," but again he stated that he thought I could do it. "So, would you like to have a go?", he asked, and I replied, "Well, if you think so!"

▶ MAS OYAMA SEEMED VERY GOOD AT ENCOURAGING PEOPLE TO TEST THEIR LIMITS.

Yes, but he also formed a judgment of my character. He knew that in my training, I would give nothing but my best. And he knew that if he gave me something to do I would work at it. In any case, he asked me and I said yes. I spoke to my wife about it and she said, "You're crazy!" I told her it would take a lot of training. At that time, my wife was working in a bank and she supported me. Without her, I would never have been able to do it.

So I started to train and it became quite a lonely life. I made my own program up with the help of Oyama. I was up very early in the morning, running up and down hills, a lot of physical training, and working out in the park. Weekends I would go down to the beach and run like hell in the sand.

▶ AND THIS WAS ON TOP OF YOUR NORMAL DOJO TRAINING?

On top of my normal dojo training. You know, Mas Oyama didn't say, "Have a break!" But he would monitor me all the time. Then I asked, "When am I going to do it?" He replied, "I'll tell you when. You just work. Don't worry about when you'll do it. Maybe you won't do it." So I kept training, training, and he kept monitoring me, checking my condition, watching me in the dojo, and this went on for six months until I was extraordinarily fit. I breathed, eat, and slept karate. Nothing else.

Then one Sunday morning when I went training as normal, I walked in, and I sensed something different. I opened the dojo doors and they were all sitting there. Oyama Sensei said, "You fight today." I didn't have any time to think about it. And then he said, "Do you accept the 100-man kumite?" I said, "Hai! Yes, I accept the challenge!" So then they phoned my wife to tell her and ask her to pick me up later. Then the fighting started, approximately a minute and a half each fight.

▶ THIS WAS CONTACT?

Yes, contact. The only thing was, my opponents couldn't kick me in the legs, but I could kick them in the legs. And no face punches were allowed. If you could knock a man down and he couldn't get up, then the fight would finish and that would help you by cutting down your fighting time. Otherwise, you did the full minute and a half. And then it was "*yame*" and the next one would get up, then the next one, and the next one. I was able to knock quite a few people down, but it would be ridiculous to say I beat everybody. The object is not to win every fight.

The object is to have the character and condition to stand and fight, to go on. If I'm in charge and you reach a point where you don't know if you are coming or going, I will stop the fighting, and I have done this in many countries. But if you are in the condition to fight, you are allowed to keep on fighting.

So, I survived the 100-man fight. I fought from green belts, brown belts and upwards, and you couldn't say I was treated kindly, because if Mas Oyama had thought one of the fighters was going easy on me he would have said to cancel the fight, so it wouldn't have counted. For them to have been easy on me would have been terrible, so I said to them to come at me strongly, for my sake. And they all played ball and they all fought hard. I was treated fairly all the way through.

You lose count of the fights. You get to a point where you feel your body's going to break up, and then it's purely your mind. So I just fought and fought and fought, and then when Okada came in, and then Shigeru, and then Nakamura Tadashi, I realized it must be getting close to the hundred. When I fought Tadashi he went hard, because he is that kind of man. He's not there to please you, he's there to give you credibility. And after that Oyama gave the order to finish and he said, "You have completed the 100-man kumite." And I shouted, "Yaaagh!" and then, "Uss!" I just stood there, and they all got up and gave me a big clap. It's an inner family affair.

Top: Steve Arneil (right) during the 100-man kumite.
Bottom: Arneil drives his attacker into the sitting crowd.

    Oyama said, "Take him down and wash him." They took me away, I was covered in blood, and my body was so sore. They washed me clean, and I could see the bruising all over my body. By the time I came back, I saw my wife was sitting there. She looked at me and her expression told me everything. Then they had a bit of a speech, we had some sake. They told me I'd done a wonderful job and they were all proud of me. Oyama put his arm around me and said, "I said you could do it. I'm glad my judgment was good." I said that I was glad I'd accomplished what he wanted me to do. He said, "I think you must now go home with your wife." I said, "I think so too," and that was it.

I walked out with my wife and I walked off as if nothing was wrong, but once I got away from the vicinity of the dojo, I almost collapsed! My wife helped me, she must have carried me back to the station and then our place. And when I got home and undressed, my God, I looked at myself and I looked like a leopard with all the bruising. My wife helped me with the bath and got me ready and I just lay there. And on the Tuesday, I was expected to train again, which I did. I trained very slow, very easy; it was quite painful, but I did it.

That was the 100-man kumite, and it was kept quiet for a long time. I just did something that Oyama wanted me to do. And then it suddenly came out at one of the World Tournaments. It was in the magazine that I was the first man to have accomplished it.

Celebration of Steve Arneil's 100-man fight.
Oyama is seated at the table. Arneil is standing. Kurosaki Kenji is at the left.

▶ YOU MUST FEEL PROUD OF THAT.

I was very proud. But you know, I hear stories about it, and I always say if you ever want to hear about it, speak to me. I'm the one who did it.

▶ THERE'S A STORY THAT MAS OYAMA DID A 300-MAN KUMITE.

I've heard that story too, but I can't confirm if it's true or not.

▶ DID YOU HEAR ABOUT IT WHEN YOU WERE IN JAPAN?

No, I didn't hear about it then. I knew he'd fought quite a lot of people, but I didn't know anything about numbers or anything. To me the 100-man kumite was just something he wanted me to do, because he said he'd done a lot of fights many years ago.

▶ DID THE KYOKUSHINKAI AT THAT TIME HAVE CONTESTS WITH OTHER STYLES?

No. We never had contests with other styles. It was an internal affair between Kyokushin dojos. At that time, the style was growing quite big in Japan, and myself and Nakamura Tadashi were in charge of Tachikawa. It was an American base, and that's how we got into the American scene. We used to go there alternately and teach.

▶ WERE YOU THERE WHEN KUROSAKI, NAKAMURA, AND FUJIHIRA WENT TO FIGHT IN THAILAND?

I was training. I was part of that squad. Myself and Oyama Shigeru's brother Yasuhiko were down to go. It was myself, Fujihira, Nakamura and Yasuhiko. I've got a few photos of when we were training. We went to a hut by the river, and we used to run in the water and train, train, train. And then, as it turned out, the squad was whittled down to Nakamura and Fujihira. I had visa problems, and I had to work, and it was difficult. And at that time, Yasuhiko had to complete his law examinations, so it was left to Nakamura and Fujihira.

▶ FUJIHIRA BECAME A KICK BOXER LATER.

That's right. After the break with Kurosaki Kenji, he left with Kurosaki and started kick boxing, which he did very successfully.

Mas Oyama (left) and his wife (far right)
at Steve Arneil's wedding.

▸ WHAT WAS HE LIKE? WAS HE A HARD TRAINER?

Fujihira was a small man, shorter than I was, but what a character. What determination! The only way to stop him would be to put a bullet between his eyes [laughing]! That's the only way I can explain it. Oh man, when he was training in the dojo!

▸ HE HAD A VERY STRONG PHYSIQUE TOO.

For his size, he was close to perfect. He was really good, and he trained religiously. You see, the problem with those two was when they were training, we had to do it with them to keep their level up, and we really had to work hard.

How it all happened—the Thai boxers sent out a challenge. They said the Japanese were sissies, they couldn't punch their way out of a paper bag, and so on. They said, "Who will challenge us?" and it was turned down by everyone. Then Mas Oyama said, "I'll challenge you!" So we all went, "Ohhh," because when he said he would challenge the Thais, we knew it would be one of us who would have to go!

In any case, they went to Thailand and they did a very good job. Fujihira won superbly, and so did Nakamura. Kurosaki, as I said, myself and Yasuhiro were suppose to go, but circumstances prevented us. But it was billed for three Japanese fighters, so the Thais said they expected another person to fight. So Kurosaki fought, and you know he shouldn't have fought. But out of courtesy, he fought and he was beaten. He got a broken nose and that type of thing. But as far as we were concerned, our boys had won by taking two out of three. And that's when we got respect from the Thai boxers.

▸ WHEN WAS IT THAT KUROSAKI LEFT KYOKUSHINKAI?

It wasn't so long after that. There was some dispute that I don't know about. Kurosaki spoke to me and said, "Look, I have to leave, and Fujihira will be leaving with me. It is up to you to make your own decision." I said, "Thank you." He then said, "Whatever decision you make it will not harm our friendship in any way." And of course he did go, and I stayed along with Nakamura and all the others.

▸ THAT MUST HAVE BEEN A BIG LOSS FOR THE DOJO.

Oh yes, it was a big loss. It was a sad time. But life must continue, and I'm sure Mas Oyama felt it as badly as we did. He never showed it, but I'm sure he felt it. Kurosaki was the first of the top men to leave. Why he left, I don't know, but there's something within Kyokushinkai that when you reached a top level like that, something—I don't know, I can't explain. It's happened to me, it's happened to Nakamura Tadashi, it's happened to Oyama Shigeru. Possibly it was politics [with Kurosaki], but at that time, I didn't know.

Kurosaki Kenji (left) shown training Fujihira Akio.

KYOKUSHINKAI IN ENGLAND

▸ OKAY, SO YOU CAME TO ENGLAND IN 1965?

Yes, in 1965, at Mas Oyama's request, as I said earlier. I met up with Bob Boulton, and we opened up the first dojo at the London Judo Society, which became the London Karatekai.

▸ THAT WAS IN THE EARLY DAYS OF KARATE IN GREAT BRITAIN?

That's right, it was very early. That was the time Suzuki and Enoeda had just arrived. Those years were just spent building up the organization.

▸ WAS IT HARD?

It was hard, but in a way, it was good too, because the training I was doing was fantastic. People liked it, but if I did that same training today, I'd have no one in the dojo.

▶ HAS KARATE CHANGED A LOT SINCE THEN?

Oh yes, things have changed. But, many people ask me how would my students of those years do now. And I have to be honest and say I think they'd get slaughtered, because of the new techniques and training methods that have come in. Where they would win, though, would be in pure determination, spirit. But the technical ability has improved so much with different training methods, and new ways of doing things. I myself was always keen to learn as much as I could from everybody else, and adapt it if I felt it would work for us. And this is the way Kyokushin in Britain developed, but never, ever did I break away from the traditions: the basics, the katas, and the strict discipline of fighting. If you fought somebody and you didn't have the decency to shake his hand afterwards, then don't bloody well fight. And this is the way I still look at my people. And this is why at our championships, if I hear one boo, I am on the microphone immediately to the crowd. It is the worst discourtesy to show to two fighters. If a fighter has made an infringement, then the referees are there to handle it, not people standing up in the crowd and booing.

▶ IN THOSE DAYS, THE 1960S AND EARLY 1970S, BRITISH KARATE SEEMED TO BE MORE TOGETHER. IN NATIONAL CHAMPIONSHIPS, ALL THE MAJOR STYLES TOOK PART.

Yes, the good old BKCC (British Karate Control Commission) Championships.

▶ SOME OF YOUR STUDENTS FOUGHT IN THEM, BRIAN FITKIN FOR EXAMPLE.

Ah, Brian Fitkin was a brilliant Kyokushinkai man. A good student, and even to this day, I still think very fondly of Brian. But at that time we weren't doing what we are doing now, knock-down fighting, or let's call it the Kyokushinkai way of fighting. We were doing...and this was very difficult for me...point fighting or you could say WUKO (World Union of Karate Organizations) type fighting. I wasn't too happy with the idea, but I knew that if I was to survive in this country and promote Kyokushin, I would have to fall into line. I was taught by my teacher to be adaptable, which I was. So I continued to train the way we'd always trained, but I added also the WUKO form of fighting and we became very successful at it. And I was very, very honored when I was approached and asked if I would become the manager of the British karate team. I thought that was fantastic and I said yes, I would like to be, because I also thought it would be a very good opportunity to also get Kyokushinkai known, because I'm a Kyokushinkai man. And it happened at that time that I had in the team—not because they were from my organization—good Kyokushinkai men like Brian Fitkin, Ticky Donovan (because he was Kyokushinkai then), Howard Collins, and various other boys who showed tremendous effort as Kyokushinkai students.

Brian, I would have to say, was the best as far as our WUKO representatives were concerned. He once fought knockdown in Japan, but not thereafter. He concentrated mainly on WUKO. And to me, he was the prize. He was like a stalking tiger. He was brilliant. If he had put his heart into knockdown, he would have been the same in that.

▸ Howard Collins fought knockdown in Japan, didn't he?

Oh, Howard Collins was brilliant as a Kyokushinkai fighter. He did very well. A tremendous fighter.

▸ The British karate squad was very strong at that time.

After a lot of hard work, and by having an open mind, we built up a very powerful squad from all styles, and that was a tremendous experience for me as they also helped me improve my knowledge in all styles.

▸ You had some good fighters.

I'll put my head on the block. I would say my team that won the World Championships, if I could get them today, at the same age, the same level, they would beat the teams now. They were brilliant: Bob Poynton, Terry O'Neill, Stan Knighton, Ticky Donovan, Hamish Adams, Billy Higgins, Brian Fitkin! I'm sorry if I've forgotten some names, but they were great, and they came from all styles. I managed to get them into believing we were one team. It didn't matter what style they came form, we were a British team, and I bred that into them all the time.

And, of course, we beat the Japanese in Paris [1972], which they weren't too happy about, and I told Kanazawa at the time—because he was their manager—"When we meet you again, we'll become the World Champions." He said, "Never!", and I replied, "You watch us!" And then in Long Beach we pulled it off, and I was very happy that I could give my services to my country in this way, and help the fighters for the future. It's turned out excellently too. So far Ticky Donovan [Arneil's successor as British coach] has done a tremendous job and we are still up there, and I hope Vic Charles, who is taking over from Ticky, will continue the tradition of producing strong British teams, because I think at the moment Britain has the highest level of martial art in Europe. I'm talking of the general level. Of course, we have cowboys like everyone else, but if you take the serious practitioners, I think we are a very strong martial arts country.

KYOKUSHINKAI TOURNAMENTS

▶ AROUND 1969, THE KYOKUSHINKAI IN JAPAN HELD THEIR FIRST NATIONAL CHAMPIONSHIPS UNDER KNOCKDOWN RULES.

Yes, and soon after that we had our own tournament in this country. In 1975 there was the first World Tournament, and those years were just brilliant.

▶ CAN WE TALK ABOUT SOME OF THE FIGHTERS FROM THAT PERIOD, LIKE SATO KATSUKO, THE FIRST WORLD CHAMPION?

Big Sato!—very strong, very dedicated, definitely a world champion.

Sato Katsuaki, the first
World Kyokushinkai Champion.

▶ ROYAMA [HATSUO]?

Oh Royama. Royama and I grew up in the dojo. He was my kohai. So were people like Soeno Yoshiji, who's now head of Shidokan karate. So I was giving them a hard time. But these were all good fighters, and gentlemen, and when I say gentlemen, I mean that on a high level. Soeno was one of the best gentlemen I've ever met. Even to this day I have tremendous respect for him, his character, the way he does things.

But people like Azuma, Sato, Sampei, Ninomiya, they were all tremendous fighters. I don't think there was any fighter who didn't deserve the honors he won. Because at that time they were the kingpins; the world around them was still learning the game. And then slowly but surely Europe got stronger and stronger and the threat [to the Japanese] was there. Then the rest of the world developed and it became quite difficult for the Japanese to dominate like before, and the tournaments were no longer one-sided affairs.

▶ THERE WAS A LOT OF DISSENT FROM THE FOREIGN COUNTRIES ABOUT THE WAY SOME OF THESE TOURNAMENTS WERE RUN, ESPECIALLY THE 1991 TOURNAMENT.

This is one of the reasons I got into hot water, because for one thing I didn't like the way the draw was done. Then I didn't like the way the Japanese could overturn decisions so they went in their favor. I didn't like the conniving that went on. There were times definitely when the non-Japanese fighters were done in. They could have become World Champions.

▶ WHAT WAS WRONG WITH THE DRAW?

Well, how can you do the draw six months ahead then put in a bye for someone? And when the day of the fighting comes, the whole thing is changed. I objected to it and I always made it clear I objected. OK, we fought open weight, so you had to take what came your way. But it was so neatly arranged that the Japanese—and this is no disrespect to the Japanese fighters themselves, they were very good—the Japanese were given an edge, because they fought smaller opponents while our fighters were getting hammered by the big opponents. By the time any of our men got through, they were so beaten up, they would lose.

▶ IT WAS ALSO SAID THAT THE STRONGEST WESTERN FIGHTERS WERE MATCHED AGAINST EACH OTHER IN THE EARLY ROUNDS.

Of course. It was obvious. I don't have to tell you that. Just look at the tapes. And all this, of course, made me sad, because I never expected this to happen in Kyokushinkai. But then again, politics, sponsorships, all those kind of things were Japanese. I got into a lot of hot water because I was told personally to change a decision and I refused point blank. And I made it clear to my teacher, who I loved very much, that I would grab the microphone and I would tell the whole audience what was happening and then I would walk out. And he said, "I know you will do it, so we won't change the decision." And he smiled at me, and afterwards he said, "You still haven't changed." He respected me for that.

But I can understand his point, because he was under pressure too from many things I don't know about. But I would never be persuaded to change a decision, and I did object strongly. And so did Nakamura, and so did Oyama Shigeru. It seemed like we were just going there as puppets, for their entertainment. We didn't have a hope in hell of winning.

I always said, why don't you do the draw a week before the tournament and do it as it should be done, like we do it here? Our draw hasn't been done yet; it'll be done tonight, the evening before the tournament. But to do it six months before—they gave us all kinds of excuses, but it was just a con.

So the Western fighter would fight against the Japanese, who would be good, but the Western fighter would be better. And then the Japanese would swing the decision on weight, but before they did that, they would look at all the aspects to the thing. So if the foreigner weighed more, they would go on weight. But if it was the other way round they would decide on boards broken, if the Japanese had broken more boards. There was no consistency. They didn't follow the system, which is weights, then boards, then decision. And I was against all this, I argued and protested about it until... Well, things happened. Certain people in my own group took advantage of it, and I got put in the hot seat.

But even at that point I would not change, because Mas Oyama himself taught me to be a man, to keep to my principles, and I know that even to his last day, he would respect me for that because he said to me—obviously I can't prove it—people will have to believe me or not. He told me, "If there's anyone ever who will continue the true spirit of Kyokushinkai, it will be you." And this is my job; I will do it to the end, maybe not under the Japanese flag, but I will do it under my own flag.

Oyama being interviewed during the All-Japan Championships.
Photo courtesy of the International Karate Organization.

LEAVING MAS OYAMA

▶ You left the Kyokushinkai organization eventually. That must have been a very hard decision for you.

Oh, it was a hard decision. You know it was my life. I understand Mr. Oyama had no option. He was under a lot of pressure. But there were a lot of false reasons given as to why I left. Supposedly I wanted to take over, I wanted to play God, all kinds of things were said against me. But that's life. If you're in the hot seat, you have to take what comes. But I disputed everything they said. My object was not to override Japan. My object was to give credibility to my teacher, which he wanted. I was always excited when we did well because I was thinking, "Sosai's [the style's founder] going to be very happy." I was for him. I didn't want to be the world controller or the world president.

But some people didn't like the rules I made and they took advantage of it and finally the day came when the old man *kensoku*'d me. That meant I wasn't put out of Kyokushinkai, but I had to stay in my own dojo. I couldn't go out of my own dojo [to teach or train] and I thought that was ridiculous. When I was kensoku'd, I wrote to my teacher. I said, "You know, we've been around so many years. I grew up in front of you"—because, indirectly, he was like my father—"and you can't tell your son to stay in his room when he's thirty years old. I have done nothing at all to injure you or hurt you. All I've tried to do is give you credibility, and to compliment you on all the things you have done. I've done the best I can, and I cannot accept this." And he replied saying I had to accept it. But when I get someone who I taught from white belt phoning me up and telling me to stay in my dojo—that's enough.

Then the BKK (British Karate Kyokushinkai) made a decision, that if Japan wasn't going to change, then we weren't going to change, because we didn't feel any necessity to. We also didn't like the politics that were going on within our own committee, where members would sit on the committee and then report back to Japan without our knowledge.

Then they said they wanted branch chiefs, and we disagreed as an organization because we didn't see the necessity for branch chiefs. "Branch chiefs" I will say openly, is a gimmick for making money. You know, give me x amount of money and I'll give you a certificate and you're a branch chief. But they broke the rules, because at that time, to be a branch chief you had to have 3,000 members. Some people who became branch chiefs didn't even have five members. I don't like working that way, and the BKK and Europe had functioned very well without branch chiefs. It was country representatives, and they were responsible, with a committee, and the committee made the decisions. But, looking back at it, I can understand why branch chiefs were introduced. It's the domino effect: if one doesn't do it, the next one will. And this is really where Mr. Oyama and myself came to the end of the line. I knew he felt very sad about it, but he was in a position where he had made a decision, and if it looked as if he had gone back on that decision—which I knew he wanted to do very badly—he would have lost face. To me "face" doesn't mean anything, but that is the Japanese way.

Then, finally, I went to Switzerland, where he was supposed to be going. I thought this would be our last consultation, but he didn't turn up. I wanted to meet openly, in front of everybody, so no one would be making up stories. And I feel I was treated badly, after all I had done, because the mandate that the other groups had given me to take to Japan about the fighting and all that—they had all signed it, yet when it came for them to support me, they didn't do it. I never ended up going to Japan. I resigned as European President, and I resigned from Kyokushinkai Headquarters.

And that is when the IFK was created, because I was inundated by people who had the same kind of thinking as I had, who had the same type of problems. They were all ex-Kyokushinkai. I thought, this is crazy, to take this all on at my time of life. But then I thought, why not. Oyama said I must always follow the Kyokushinkai principles, and so I decided I'd do it.

▶ HOW BIG IS THE IFK NOW?

It's big. We've got over twenty countries and we've only been in existence four or five years. We're doing our first world tournament in Moscow next year. It's a healthy organization, but what will take place in the future, nobody knows. My ambition is to create some happiness and the proper spirit of budo.

▶ THERE ARE NOW A LOT OF KYOKUSHIN OR KYOKUSHIN-OFFSHOOT GROUPS IN THE WORLD, LIKE OYAMA SHIGERU'S, NAKAMURA'S, AND SO ON.

Yes, but often they have done what I haven't done. When people ask me what style I do, I say "Kyokushin." I haven't changed the style. Oyama Shigeru has the World Oyama style, and he has changed it in line with his ideas. Nakmura Tadashi has his Seido style, and he has changed certain things, although obviously there's a lot of Kyokushin in it. Soeno of Shidokan, he has changed some things. I haven't. I keep Kyokushin techniques and I am a Kyokushin man. The old man made me a Kyokushin man. I took it very seriously when he said I would be a Kyokushinkai man all my life.

What I do know is that if Oyama were alive today, he would be a very, very sad man. He didn't want it to be like this. He wanted a healthy family. He wanted something with credibility. He wanted people to say, "Hey, they're Kyokushinkai. They're a strong group." It was never his intention that things would turn out the way they did, but in a way, he should take some of the blame. He didn't listen to people who loved him very much. I want to keep that spirit of Kyokushin. To me it was beautiful. I was a wild boy when I was young, and I don't know where I'd have been without Kyokushin. So I want to give something back. But no way will I be untrue to my principle—otherwise, what was it all for?

Steve Arneil.

And I want to say, if it wasn't for my good students and a lot of good people around me, I couldn't have accomplished it. So I thank all my students, all my executives and all my coaches for what we've achieved.

References

Nakamura, T. (1989). *The human face of karate*. New York: World Seido Karate Organization.

Oyama, M. (1966, 1973). *This is karate*. Tokyo: Japan Publications Inc.

Oyama, M. (1973). *This is karate*. NY: Wehman Brothers.

Oyama, M. (1958). *What is karate?* Tokyo: Japan Publications Trading.

Oyama, M. (1966). *What is karate?* NY: HarperCollins.

chapter 3

The Legacy of Dr. Richard Kim: An Interview with Brian Ricci

by Robert Toth

Left: Richard Kim with Yoshida Kotaro.
Right: Dr. Kim demonstrating a technique with sickles.

Introduction

As an artist uses different medium such as clay, paint, or music as a means of artistic expression, a martial artist uses his own life (Kim, 1988). Richard Kim was such an artist. His completed artistic work, his life, went far beyond what most people could ever hope to imagine, let alone accomplish. If the student must surpass the teacher to pay his debt to him, then Richard Kim set the bar very, very high. He was a boxer, soldier, priest (Warrener, n.d.), Ph.D. in oriental philosophy (Warrener, 1982: 65), writer and lecturer, linguist who spoke six languages (Ricci, 2005, May 17), and a martial arts teacher (*sensei*).

Sensei is a term meaning "teacher" or "instructor" used in all Japanese and Okinawan arts. It is written in Japanese with two characters, *sen* (before) and *sei* (life). Within the martial arts context, the sensei is a person with considerable experience of life, some from the normal course of living and some from the martial arts (Castilonia, 1996: 143, 144).

Sensei are charged with developing their students to the highest potential and are considered pointers of the Way (*do*) (Sells 2000: 369). Sensei are responsible for overseeing the training and personal development of their students. They command absolute respect and authority. The students, in return, accept their sensei's authority and follow his teachings without question (Wingate, 1993: 24).

The sensei must constantly exemplify the highest standards of martial art discipline, the whole idea of which is to develop character. The martial Way must be the sensei's way of life, and he must give himself completely to his art in order to pass on the full range of that art's teaching to his students (McCarthy, 1987: 10). Dr. Kim was an exemplary sensei.

A Brief Overview of Dr. Kim's Life Story

Dr. Richard Kim.

Richard Kim was born in Hawai'i on 17 November 1919 of a Korean father and Japanese mother (Warrener, 1982: 91). His father was a landscaper and his mother owned a hotel (Ricci, 2005, May 4). The basement of the hotel was rented to judo instructor Tachibana. When Richard was six years old, his mother enrolled him in judo classes (Warrener, n.d.).

Kim's karate training began in 1927 with Arakaki Ankichi (1899-1927), a disciple of Yabu Kentsu (Kim, 1974: 3). Yabu Kentsu had been a student of two great Okinawan karate masters, Matusumura Sokon and Itosu Yasutsune. Yabu was one of the first men to teach martial arts in the Okinawan school system and was known as "The Sergeant" (McCarthy, 1987: 32). In 1927, on his way back to Okinawa after a visit to California, Yabu stopped over in Hawai'i. He gave a demonstration at the Nuuanu YMCA on 8 July 1927 (Svinth, 2001: 10, 14). After seeing the demonstration, Richard Kim started training in Yabu's Shorinji-ryu style (Warrener, n.d.), which is a synthesis of Okinawan and Japanese karate (Farkas and Corcoran, 1983: 242). In the 1930's, Kim met Yabu Kentsu again in Japan and continued training with him (Ricci, 2005, April 21).

"Biggie" Kim, as he was known, spent a great deal of time as a teenager at local boxing clubs, where he acquired boxing skills by acting as a sparring partner for some of the top world contenders (Kim, 1982: 6, 7). He later explained what he learned most from boxing was the jab and focus. He also learned the limitations of boxing when he witnessed a Hall of Fame lightweight boxer driven head first into the floor by a Samoan (Ricci, 2005, April 21). Kim had 42 fights in the ring and became the champion of the Orient while living in Shanghai (Warrener, 2001: 93).

After graduating from high school, Kim attended the University of Hawai'i. At the university, he joined the Reserve Officers Training Corp (ROTC) and was made a captain. Men who completed the training were given commissions in the US Army Reserve (www.hawaii.edu/armyrotc).

In 1939, Kim arranged to travel to Japan by working on a ship in lieu of payment (Warrener, n.d.). He was able to go to Japan because he had been born prior to the Exclusions Act of 1924 and held dual citizenship (Warrener 2001: 93). But upon arrival, he had to "jump ship" because he was underage (Ricci, 2005, April 21). Once in Japan, Kim became a member of the Japanese military (Warrener 2001: 92).

In Japan, Kim trained with Yoshida Kotaro in Daito-ryu aikijutsu (Warrener, n.d.). Daito-ryu was one of the most renowned of the old Japanese styles of combat and had been practiced by Minamoto clan warriors for several centuries before the Takeda family inherited it (Ratti and Westbrook, 1973: 356). Kotaro had trained with Takeda Sokato (Warrener, n.d.).

Yoshida Kotaro was renowned for his weapon skills (Sells, 2000: 135, 137) and was an expert with the spear (*yari*) and the glave (*naginata*) (Corcoran, et al., 1993: 396). The training with Yoshida Kotaro was very physical and very harsh. Kotaro taught throwing techniques and also worked with swords and knives. Kim became an apprentice under Kotaro and eventually was given the Daito-ryu *menkyo kaiden* (Warrener, 2001: 92). Menkyo kaiden is a certificate that attests to a student's full proficiency and is usually awarded to the advanced student deemed most suited to carry on the art (Farkas and Corcoran, 1983: 177).

Richard Kim was then sent to China as an interpreter for a Japanese Imperial Army officer (Ricci Dec.12, 2005). Here he had the opportunity to study martial arts. Chen Chin-wan taught him a slightly modified version of Yang style taijiquan. He learned baguazhang with Chao Hsu-lie whom he met while in Hong Kong. Kim also trained in Yiquan gongfu with Wang Xiangzhai (1885/6-1963). His first lesson was to stand in a qigong posture known as "embrace the tree" for three hours a day (Warrener, n.d.). While living in Shanghai, Kim also attended St. John's University (Kim, 1982: 6-7).

After World War II, Kim owned and operated a bar in Yokohama, Japan. Mas Oyama and Kinjo Hiroshi would come by his house once a week to train. He later met Yamaguchi Gogen through Oyama (Warrener, n.d.). During this period, Kim represented the Seaman's Union in Yokohama (Kim, 1999).

In 1959, Kim moved to San Francisco, California (Kim, 1974: 3). He conducted a martial arts program at the Chinese YMCA until his semi-retirement in 1978. Over the years, Dr. Kim traveled all over the world teaching the martial arts. He created a large international organization, the Zen Bei Butokukai, with schools in the US, Canada, and Europe. *Zen Bei* literally translates as "All Rice." Japanese characters, however, can have multiple meanings, depending on the context. The character for "rice" can refer to "people in general." So, Zen Bei can also be translated as "All People" (Foley, 2005, July 3).

In 2000, the Hawai'i Karate Kodanshakai awarded Dr. Kim a tenth-degree black belt (Goodin, 2005). In the same year at a gathering held in a Chinese restaurant in Sacramento, Dr. Kim told the group that he had awarded a seventh-degree ranking to his longtime student, Brian Ricci. That was the only time he had conferred that rank on anyone. It was the highest dan ranking he had ever given (Ricci, 2005, May 22).

Dr. Kim demonstrating
a boxing technique in Hamilton, Ontario.

Kim Sensei did not attend the annual Zen Bei Butokukai 2001 Summer Camp held at Guelph University in Ontario, Canada, because of poor health. He arranged for Brian Ricci to run the camp in his absence. At a black belt meeting on the first evening of the summer camp, Ricci explained that he had expected that some day Kim Sensei would not be able to teach, but had hoped it would not have been so soon. Ricci made it clear that he had been put in charge of the camp and he intended to fulfill his responsibility to his sensei.

Richard Kim died on 8 November 2001. Brian Ricci has continued his teacher's work in propagating the martial arts. The majority of Kim Sensei's students now train with Ricci Sensei. The Zen Bei Butokukai International Summer Camp at Guelph University continues to be held every year and has grown under Ricci Sensei's care with students attending from all over North America.

BRIAN RICCI INTERVIEW

Dr. Kim with Brian Ricci.

The following interview with Brian Ricci Sensei was conducted by Robert Toth on 21 April 2005 in St. Catharines, Ontario.

▸ WHEN AND WHERE WERE YOU BORN?

I was born on August 14, 1950 in Everett, Massachusetts, six miles from downtown Boston. Today, I live a half a mile from where I was born.

▸ WHEN DID YOU FIRST BECOME INVOLVED WITH THE MARTIAL ARTS AND WHY?

I've always been a movie buff. Watching Jimmy Cagny doing judo in *Blood on the Sun* or the Mr. Moto movies. Nobody knew what karate was back then, but I knew I wanted to learn how to do those techniques.

It was about 1962 when I went to my mother and said that I'd like to learn jujutsu. She told me to get a book. When I was about 14, I told her that I wanted to learn karate. She said that she didn't want to have anyone in the house who knew how to kill people [laughs]. But in 1965, I had to have a chest operation. When I was leaving the hospital in a cast my dad asked, "Any wish?" I could have anything I wanted. So, I told him I wanted to take karate. From the hospital he took me to a karate school. Then on 15 March, after I healed, I started at a Shotokan karate school.

▸ WHO WAS YOUR FIRST INSTRUCTOR? DID YOU GET YOUR BLACK BELT FROM HIM?

Peter Ventresca. Yes, I got my black belt from him in 1972.

▸ YOU DON'T MAKE YOUR LIVING WITH MARTIAL ARTS INSTRUCTION. WHAT ALL DO YOU DO?

I do a number of different things. A lot of things in the movie industry. Stunts and special effects. When I first moved to California, I was living at the YMCA. I heard fire engines and I went out to see what was going on. They were filming the movie *Towering Inferno*. I met the wardrobe man for the movie and at one point he said to me, "just walk over there." If you look at the *Towering Inferno* video, near the end of the movie you'll see me walking past behind the actors. Much later I was doing a martial arts demonstration and a fellow came over and asked me if I could coordinate the same kind of thing for special effects in the theater.

If you read the introduction I wrote for Sensei Kim's book, *The Classical Man* [1982], you'll see how I feel about teaching martial arts for a living.

▸ WHEN DID YOU FIRST MEET SENSEI KIM?

I was 23 years old and it was July 1973. I had been training with Luis DeBacario for about two years. I wanted to learn in more depth, so I sent Sensei Kim a letter. He sent word back that I could train and that was it. I decided to quit my job and drove my 1969 Buick from Boston to San Francisco. I arrived at Sensei's dojo and he asked me how I got there. I told him I drove. He said, "You drove?" I said, "Yes. My car's parked out front." He said, "Not anymore." And when I looked they had towed my car [laughs]! I didn't know the law about parking on the street.

▸ WHAT WAS THE TRAINING LIKE WITH SENSEI KIM THEN?

There was vigorous repetition. For months there was no katas [forms], just kick, punch, tiger bends, stretching. Then he told me to come to the summer camp in San Diego. He taught five or six katas in one week. In my background, we learned maybe one kata a year. Sensei asked, "How can you learn the advanced kata without knowing the basic kata?"

▸ WHAT DID SENSEI KIM TEACH AT THE CHINESE YMCA?

Tuesday and Thursday was taiji. Monday, Wednesday, and Saturday was sparring, free style with takedowns, then we'd do mat work from there. And the staff [*bo*]. Just drill and drill.

Sensei Kim always used the words "martial arts." He said karate had limits. You had to become an artist of life.

▸ OVER THE YEARS, YOU MUST HAVE SEEN MANY PEOPLE COME AND GO. HOW DID YOUR RELATIONSHIP AND YOUR POSITION WITH SENSEI KIM CHANGE?

At first I only saw him from across the room. I was invisible. Then in France in 1975, he said to me, "Now I know who to travel with." And I was never excluded. Over time that developed into my being the assistant instructor on the road. He would take me into his confidence and he'd ask, "What should we teach?" I was honored that he'd seek my opinion. Finally, it was, "Brian, run this event."

One of his greatest compliments was when he introduced me to someone in Sacramento. He said, "Rose, meet my friend, Brian Ricci." I was taken back that he'd call me his friend.

Dr. Kim demonstrates sai techniques.

▸ WHY WAS RECEIVING A DAN RANK FROM SENSEI KIM SO SPECIAL?

I came from a Shotokan background. Frank Gaviola was from a different background. We felt we were somewhat accomplished martial artists. But to have recognition from Sensei Kim was difficult to earn. The first degree [*shodan*] and second degree [*nidan*] were working ranks. There were very few third degrees [*sandans*]. Other organizations out there had sixth and seventh degrees that were nowhere near as good as Sensei Kim's black belts. I was a fourth degree for many years. The fourth-dan relationship was different. It meant you were self-sufficient. He wanted to know everything about you. Sensei Kim knew your personality. He knew your moral code in life.

I never asked him for rank. When Sensei Kim sent me the seventh degree, I never told anyone. He announced it at the banquet to celebrate his 80th birthday and his tenth-degree.

Brian Ricci adjusting sai technique under his mentor.

▶ What is your fondest memory of Sensei Kim?

Sensei's sense of humor. His laugh. We loved to get him going. I remember the summer camp the first time we did a little magic thing called "The Stubby Shapiro Show." It was based on a joke that Sensei had told. But, that day something had ticked off Sensei Kim. He really wasn't in a good mood. But because of the show, Sensei Kim laughed so hard he had tears in his eyes. And I felt so good that we could do something like that to change his mood.

▶ What is the most important thing that you learned from Sensei Kim?

Be happy. Enjoy life each day. Live in the moment.

▶ The majority of Sensei Kim's students are now training with you. What legacy of Sensei Kim's are you trying to pass on to them?

Tradition. Sensei Kim said that if it comes easy, it doesn't have value. Martial arts tradition has been around for a long time.

▶ Can you tell us about the Zen Bei Butokukai International?

Sensei Kim chose the name Zen Bei Butokukai International. As Zen Bei means "all people," it reflects his reaching out to everyone. The shape of the crest we use is purely a respect for Sensei Kim.

After Sensei Kim's passing he had left no written instructions as to how things were to continue. But, I like to think it worked out for the best.

▸ WHAT DO YOU SEE FOR YOUR FUTURE IN THE MARTIAL ARTS?

I enjoy being a vehicle to pass on Sensei Kim's teaching and develop his students to the best of their abilities and to treat all students with fairness and keep his level of teaching.

▸ IS THERE ANYTHING ELSE YOU'D LIKE TO SAY?

We all looked at Sensei Kim as a flawless individual. I got to know him as the man. He made mistakes. But his generosity was to a fault. He always made sure his students got the best.

Dr. Kim was in the true sense a sensei: "One who has gone before" and shares his knowledge with students.

TECHNICAL SECTION

The prototypes of the spear (*yari*) were originally brought to Japan from the Asian continent and enjoyed their greatest popularity after the Mongol invasions of the late 13th century (Draeger, 1973: 71, 72). To the Japanese warrior (samurai), the spear was second only to the bow and arrow in traditional significance (Ratti and Westbrook, 1973: 241). Even though elaborate spearhead designs took the spear out of the category of piercing weapons and gave it new roles in slashing, hooking, and ripping, the basic mechanics of the spear art continued unchanged and the Japanese samurai trained primarily to be accurate with the thrust (Draeger, 1973: 72).

It is interesting to note that the staff (*bo*) was developed at the same time as the art of spear fighting and the boundaries between the two arts have become rather vague. The staff was comparatively less dangerous to practice with than a spear and was often used in the martial art training halls (*dojo*) where spear fighting was taught. In time, the related use of the wooden weapon became so well developed that skilled warriors could be engage in real combat using the staff (Ratti and Westbrook, 1973: 305, 308).

Although the Japanese have used wooden weapons since earliest times, the staff was a humble weapon, because the lowliest person could make one. Because of its obvious effectiveness, however, the samurai could not afford to neglect its study (Draeger, 1973: 76).

Yoshida Kotaro was known as a spear expert (Corcoran, et al., 1993: 396) and Kim often spoke of training with the spear under his teacher (Kim, 1982: 35, 77, 82, 89). Ricci explained many of the kata practiced with the staff that have been passed down from Kim Sensei and taught in the Zen Bei Butokukai are actually spear forms (B. Ricci, 2005, April 21). The kata, *Yunigawa no kon*, was originally meant to be performed with the spear (B. Ricci, 2005, May 24).

The opening movements of Yunigawa no kon.

Brian Ricci demonstrates a combination from the Yunigawa no kon. The second move is a retraction of the bo in order to thrust under the opponents block.

Blocking
with the yari or bo
is done with the shaft.

Thrust and retract.

It is important to use a proper grip with the yari/bo. If the palm is up the weapon can be dislodged with a strike.

The palm must be down in order to have control of the weapon.

Thrusting with the yari/bo is with a twisting motion. Here Brian Ricci uses a training technique taught by his sensei, Dr. Richard Kim. Dr. Kim had his students use a wet towel to thrust into to show the twisting of the yari/bo.

Conclusion

No one ever will replace Dr. Richard Kim. The circumstances of his life gave him the opportunity to train in a number of martial arts in the countries of their origin during turbulent times. His personal development was a result of his amazing work ethic. Dr. Kim once said, "If you sleep more than four hours a day, you lose."

Today, four years after his death, Dr. Kim's students are faced with the daunting task of passing on their instructor's teachings. Their loyalty and devotion guarantee Dr. Kim's knowledge and wisdom will continue into the next generation. And that generation is sure to view the stories of this great man's life as legend.

Acknowledgment

The author would like to thank Brian Ricci Sensei for providing some of the photographs used in this chapter. A special thanks to both Ricci Sensei and Frank Gaviola Sensei for their help and suggestions with the chapter. Great appreciation is expressed as well to Ed Ricci, John Wasilina, Dean and Tony Romanelli, and Kelly Combs for appearing in the photos. The author would especially like to thank Dr. Richard Kim for his guidance.

Notes

[1] Oyama Masutatsu was born Yee Hyung in Kimje, Korea in 1923. In 1937, he was sent to a boy's military academy in Japan. He changed his name and began studying Shotokan karate. After the war, Oyama studied Goju-ryu karate and eventually created his own style, Kyokushinkai (Corcoran, et al., 1993: 365)

[2] Kinjo Hiroshi was born on Valentines Day, 1919. He originally trained in the marital arts with Hanashiro Chomo (1869-1945) and Oshiro Chojo (1888-1935) in Okinawa (McCarthy, 1994: 91).

[3] Yamaguchi Gogen was born on 20 January 1909. As a boy, he trained in Japanese fencing (*kendo*) and karate. In 1931, he was introduced to the founder of Goju-ryu karate, Miyagi Chojun (Yamaguchi, n.d.: 75-77, 84).

[4] *Butokukai* means "Martial Virtues Association" (Draeger 1974: 35).

[5] Frank Gaviola began training with Richard Kim in 1968 at the YMCA in San Francisco's Chinatown. He received his sixth-degree black belt in 2001. He received his associate's degree in architectural engineering from City College of San Francisco. After a 25-year career in engineering, he quit work to teach martial arts full-time in 1992 (Gould, 2002: 22).

Bibliography

Castilonia, R. (1996). *Nuggets in the ground.* LaJolla, CA: International University Line.

Corcoran, J., Farkas, E., and Sobel, S. (1993). *The original martial arts encyclopedia: Tradition-history-pioneers.* Los Angeles: ProAction Publishing.

Draeger, D. (1973). *Classical bujutsu.* Tokyo: Weatherhill Inc.

Draeger, D. (1974). *Modern bujutsu and budo.* Tokyo: Weatherhill Inc.

Farkas, E., and Corcoran, J. (1983). *The Overlook martial arts dictionary.* New York: The Overlook Press.

Foley, S. (2005, July 3). Personal communication with author.

Gould, J. (ed.). (2002, September). Sensei spotlight: Frank Gaviola. *Martial Virtue,* 22.

Kim, R. (1974). *The weaponless warriors.* Burbank, CA: Ohara Publications.

Kim, R. (1982). *The classical man.* Hamilton, Ontario: Masters Publication.

McCarthy, P. (1987). *Classical kata of Okinawan karate.* Santa Clarita, CA: Ohara Publications.

McCarthy, P. (1994). The world within karate and Kinjo Hiroshi. *Journal of Asian Martial Arts,* 3(2): 90-99.

Ratti, O., and Westbrook, A. (1973). *Secrets of the samurai.* Rutland, VT: Charles E. Tuttle Company.

Ricci, B. (2005, April 21). Personal communication with author.

Ricci, B. (2005, May 4). Personal communication with author.

Ricci, B. (2005, May 17). Personal communication with author.

Ricci, B. (2005, May 22). Personal communication with author.

Ricci, B. (2005, May 24). Personal communication with author.

Sells, J. (2000). *Unante: The secrets of karate.* Hollywood, CA: W.M. Hawley.

Svinth, J. (2001). Karate pioneer Yabu Kentsu, 1866-1937. *Journal of Asian Martial Arts,* 10(2): 8-17.

Werrener, D. (n.d.). Memorial video–Sensei Richard Kim 1917-2001. Private production.

Warrener, D. (1982, May). Richard Kim: The weaponless warrior. *Official Karate,* 65.

Warrener, D. (2001, June). Richard Kim: The classical man. *Masters of Karate,* 93.

Will, J. (n.d.). Gogen "the cat" Yamaguchi: The last interview. *Fighter International,* 24, 26.

Wingate, C. (1993). Exploring our roots: Historical and cultural foundations of the ideology of karate-do. *Journal of Asian Martial Arts,* 2(3): 10-35.

Yamaguchi, G. (n.d.). *Karate Goju-ryu by the cat.* Tokyo: International Karate-do Goju-kai.

chapter 4

George Dillman and the Influences in Pressure Point Theory and Practice

Interview by Peter Hobart, J.D.

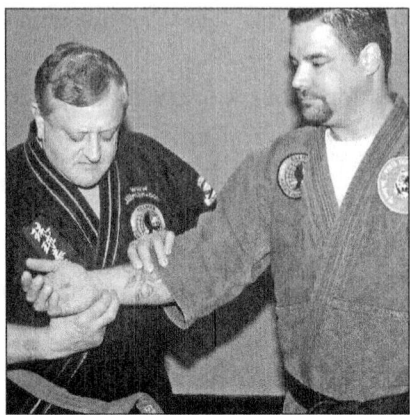

George Dillman indicating pressure points on the arm.
All photographs courtesy of George Dillman.

Almost anyone who has trained in Okinawan or Japanese martial arts over the past three decades will be familiar with the name of George A. Dillman. In 1982, he was described by *Official Karate Magazine* as "one of the winningest competitors karate has ever known" (November, 1982). He was a four-time National Karate Champion between 1969 and 1972, and during this period, he was consistently ranked among the top ten competitors in the nation by many major karate publications. Since that time, his advancement of *kyusho-jitsu* (pressure point theory) has sent shock waves through much of the martial community and turned certain traditional practices on their ear.

Volumes have been written about the technical aspects of his system. What has received somewhat less attention—perhaps eclipsed by the tremendous interest in the practicalities of the art—is an examination of the ideas, principles and beliefs that drive the man. On 21 February 2004, in Freehold, New Jersey, I had the opportunity to present him with a number of questions on such issues as history, tradition, ethics and even philosophy. What follows is a rare insight into another aspect of a man that many people already know, and perhaps others may want to take the time to get to know.

INTERVIEW

▶ PETER HOBART: PLEASE DISCUSS THE RELATIONSHIP BETWEEN PRESSURE POINT FIGHTING AND CONVENTIONAL, COMPETITIVE SPARRING.

George A. Dillman: My karate has always been geared at real self-defense —something that will work out on the street—even when I broke down my kata and forms before considering the pressure points, I kept in mind "how would this play out in a real street fight situation?" In the military (police) I was in several encounters where I had to handle some trouble situations and I realized that some of the martial arts techniques that we talked about in the dojo just wouldn't work, and I realized that early on, so I was lucky there. I feel fortunate, though, that I was a sport competitor because had I bypassed that to go into pressure points—which I would have, probably, full-on—if I would have bypassed the sport end of it, I would have lacked a basic ability that I've told people they must have.

We have people that are doing pressure point techniques today that don't compete, they don't spar, they have probably never been in a real self-defense situation and they can't defend themselves. They can learn all the pressure points in the world, but during my sport period, I learned all the things that are actually needed to deliver the pressure points in a real situation, and I developed timing, distance and coordination. If you don't freestyle spar back at your dojo, if you don't pair off and do self-defense, you can't just do pressure point techniques. You could pull one or two off, maybe, for a basic breakaway, but for full-on self-defense you need to develop timing, distance and coordination. That happens—and it happens even more so in a tournament—when the pressure is on, because you have the same pressure, if not a deeper pressure, that you would have in a street situation, because there's thousands of people yelling your name or your opponent's name.

At the same time, that's what made me look for the pressure points, that's what made me find Soken Hohan, that's what made me ask him the question, because I knew we were lacking something. In tournament competition there were several times—and this is the way it was back then, there was no safety gear—when I actually punched some people and wanted to drop them, and they didn't drop. I was told, "One punch kill," "One punch can drop the guy," and I had to be missing something. What is it? Because I just hit this man as hard as I can and they're awarding me a point. Now a point is great, but in a street fight it doesn't mean anything… If I put you in the ring with Mike Tyson and he hits you, he's going to win. You've got to avoid being hit and you've got to be able to get him, and you're going to win.

▶ Can you discuss Soken Hohan (b. 1889), Oyata Seiyu, and your first discovery of pressure point theory?

Dillman with Soken Hohan.

I realized I was missing something and I realized that there had to be something in the kata because people were now making up their own katas and forms to music, yet in the Orient they were sticking to those basic Pinan katas, Naihanchi kata, they were sticking to basic katas and teaching them and doing them with a different type of look in their eyes, using *ki* (internal energy), using rooting, using a whole different way of doing forms. I realized that, and I realized that in this country, because we didn't learn the secrets, we were making things up, and I would not fall to that. I asked Soken Hohan, and that's when he gave me the decent answers.

When I got the answers, they were somewhat depressing because I had spent twenty years learning these katas, and now all of a sudden there's no blocks, everything has a serious meaning—every move in every kata—it's just that we didn't know it, and it was right before our eyes. I was actually angry with myself, that I didn't figure it out. The real answers were right in front of my eyes and I didn't see them... I needed tournament competition to get me where I'm at today... My being good at kata is what led Soken Hohan to work with me. He said to me, "You do such beautiful kata that it hurts me here (indicating his heart) to see that you don't know the answer. You do kata even with spirit. In Okinawa we look that you have spirit to have kata. You have spirit. You just don't know what you are doing with the moves... This what you need to be a master in my country."

In 1983 I ran into Oyata Seiyu. The minute he did his first technique and said, "This is out of a kata," and broke it down, he wasn't on the mat ten seconds and I leaned over—my wife was there—and I whispered in her ear,

"That's what Soken Hohan did. This is what Soken Hohan was trying to get across. This is what my notes are about. I have notes on this—on what he's doing right now—now I'm understanding it." Oyata Seiyu gave me the keys to get in the door. I had the door, I had the path, I had the katas, I had the general idea, I knew everything was more serious, I knew there were no blocks, but I didn't know what they were.

▸ WHAT WAS IT LIKE TEACHING FOR OVER FIFTEEN YEARS IN COOPERATION WITH WALLY JAY, LEO FONG AND REMY PRESAS?

Among Dillman's associates how have influenced his martial art studies have been Bruce Lee and Muhammad Ali.

I attended those people's seminars (Wally Jay, Leo Fong, Remy Presas), I had them in to my school for seminars and we got talking about technique and we wound up sharing. From the minute I saw (Wally Jay) on the mat, I knew that I needed his Small Circle jujutsu for what I was doing. I had an Okinawan master—Oyata Seiyu—who said if you really want to find out the secret, you need a good jujutsu man. Along came Wally Jay, who was the best jujutsu man, and I realized the day he walked in the dojo that it was the Small Circle jujutsu that I was missing. I was able to hit people and hurt them, stun them, but I wasn't able to knock them out as well as I was after studying with Wally Jay. It is that Small Circle theory that he teaches and does that completed my art. He also then found that utilizing pressure points would help him complete his art. He and I used pressure point techniques, but we didn't know how they all fit together in the big package, and now we do.

So we started sharing, which led me over to Remy (Presas) and Remy came in, and he started working with me on disarming people, taking weapons away, and I worked with him on pressure point techniques. The three of us had some sessions that I would give anything to have on video. We had some training sessions with the four of us doing and sharing techniques that the average martial artist would find unbelievable. It was fantastic. Remy—I miss him greatly. I always tell people that he was my booking agent. Remy would call me. "You and I will teach a seminar. We will do this in Atlanta, Georgia." I'd ask, "We will?" He'd say, "Yes, yes, you must be there," and then he'd hang up! And he did the same thing with Wally and we put the three of us together, and that became awesome for almost fifteen years.

▸ What makes a master? How were your encounters with such people?

The ability to teach, the ability to get you to do it, there are a lot of people that are good martial artists but they're not good at teaching. Bruce Lee was amazing at getting the concept across. I only worked out with Bruce Lee three times, but he improved my hand speed. He told me right off the bat, "You have to improve your hand and foot speed. You have a lot of power, good techniques, but I can hit you three or four times before you can hit me." Then he did it! But he taught me how to do it too. Then my hand speed picked up.

Daniel K. Pai was one of the unequaled masters in the world. He had so many techniques, but he passed away at an odd time, like Remy Presas, before anyone expected it. Danny Pai was one of the best gongfu teachers at the time. When I had sessions sitting at a dinner table with Bruce Lee and Danny Pai, I just sat and listened. And I was learning more than most people learn in their lifetime in a dojo, over a dinner table. That was amazing—these people could teach by words also, then they could get up and demonstrate.

Robert Trias was one of the first Americans to do the martial arts, and he was a tremendous person and a strong puncher—you wouldn't want to be hit with his punch! I wasn't the size of Robert Trias. Trias was a big, huge strong man, so when he hit, you wouldn't want to be in front of it. But Bruce Lee wasn't, and Bruce Lee made me pay attention to speed and power, because Bruce was a small individual—he was only 5' 7", 125 pounds—so I realized that that was the answer. I just happened to be with the right people at the right time. However, a little credit goes my way because I would seek these people out; they didn't find me.

Ed Parker and I were friends—Ed Parker and Danny Pai were first cousins—and Danny Pai introduced me to Ed Parker, and Ed Parker introduced me to Bruce Lee. Bruce Lee introduced me to Wally Jay and Leo Fong. Bruce Lee sat at my house and said, "Who are some of the toughest fighters on the East Coast—I don't get over here often? Somebody who, if you were going to run into them in a real fight, you'd know you better pay attention and be using both hands." I gave him a couple of names of people I thought of at the time, that I respected and were big, strong fighters. And he took that into his memory bank. I said, "How about on the West Coast?" He said, "There are several," and named them.

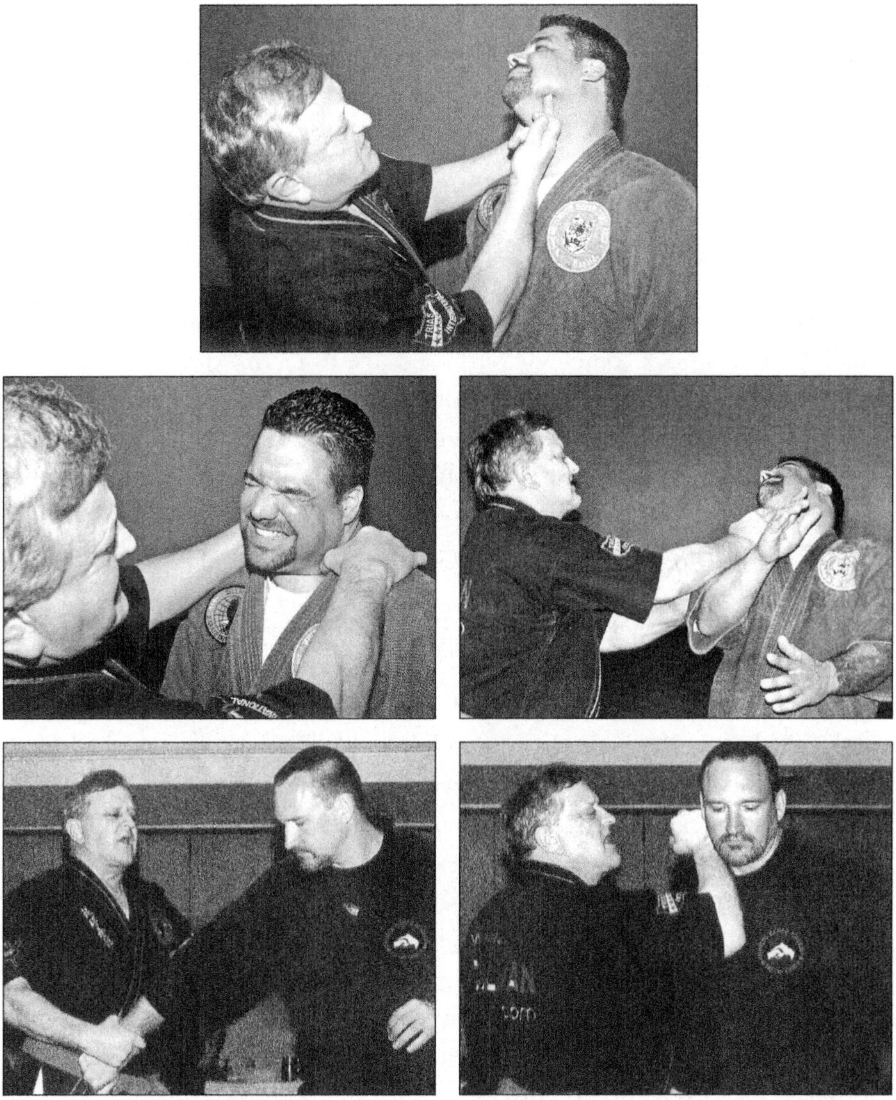

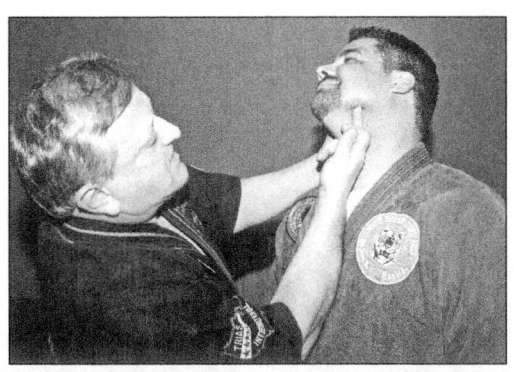

Explaining the locations of pressure points on the jaw, neck and wrist, and how theory is applicable in martial art practice.

Lee said, "there's a guy out there named Wally Jay. You've got to meet and train with Wally Jay at some point. He's a no nonsense person. You ask Wally Jay a question; he does not answer the question verbally. He gets you on the mat and demonstrates it, and you can do nothing about it. I've seen some of the best martial artists in the world get on the mat with Wally Jay, and they get defeated. You've got to train with him. Leo Fong is one of the toughest boxers I've met. You have to slug it out with him, and you have to be ready to take him down, because he will keep coming." After Bruce Lee passed away was when I went to seek out Wally Jay and Leo Fong. I went to Canada to meet with Wally Jay, and took a whole bunch of my students to watch him on the mat, doing his thing, and I approached him about doing a seminar at my school.

▶ ON THE IMPORTANCE OF STUDYING AND TEACHING HEALING ARTS IN CONJUNCTION WITH MARTIAL PRACTICES:

Three reasons. The ethical reason, the practical reason… because you as a martial artist have to learn to reverse what you learn how to do. If you hurt somebody, you knock somebody out; you have to learn how to revive them. The third reason is that I, and several other people who are into pressure point theory, are looking for ways to lengthen our lives… and I think we're finding it. We're finding better ways to restore our ki energy, we're finding ways to restore after seminars so we're not tired and weak, and that all leads to the healing part of it. We're not only healing, but we're learning the healing within ourselves.

The thing that I found is that most martial artists that are into what I'm into lived into their nineties with complete flexibility. Soken Hohan is on the end of my videotape doing forms. He was 92-years-old. That tape was shot two weeks before he died. Now he didn't know he was going to die in two weeks, but his body was winding down… What was amazing was at 92 he could do a kata called Chinto and jump in the air and throw two kicks and he could go to the ground on one knee and get up, and he could do a complete spin, 180 degrees, and not fall over. You go out and take the average man that's 92 and spin him around and he's going to fall over. Well he had complete control of his body, his energy; he knew how the energy spiraled up and down… When you spin and move in a kata, you are controlling your energy and sending it up and down through your body. If you know how to do that, it creates health and flexibility.

▶ WHAT ARE THE HUMANE ASPECTS OF KYUSHO-JITSU, THE PRESSURE POINT THEORY?

The art that I teach is a lot more humane than punching people in the Adam's apple, poking out his eye, kicking him in the groin—this is what they advise at most karate schools. They're all teaching eye gouges, they're all teaching how to cup hands and hit in both ears. They're all teaching to rip out the Adam's apple or hitting in the throat. They're all teaching how to kick in the groin. I had to go through that in my mind when I got into pressure points, because I realized how deadly they are, and could be...they're just going for what we call "vital points." Vital points like eyes, ears, nose, throat and groin. We have pressure points—there are 361 all over—we have variations to go to because you need them in various self-defense situations. You cannot always get to the eyes, ears, nose, throat and groin—they have a natural defense. There isn't anybody in the world that doesn't flinch at an eye gouge or a groin kick... There are pressure points available that give you the exact same result.

 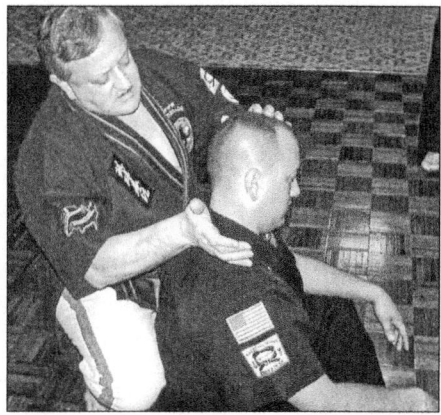

Dillman showing resuscitation techniques.

▶ WHAT IMPORTANCE DO EMOTIONS PLAY IN MARTIAL TECHNIQUE?

You read in any martial arts book—any good one—that you should be happy or complacent while fighting. Do not take the anger of your opponent. Anger negates anger. You take two people that are angry, hitting at each other, they cannot do damage to each other. Take one and get him angry, get the other one laughing and he punches the guy that's angry, the guy that's angry will fall down... I've been in several self-defense encounters and I didn't realize it, but I was happy and smiling, but I was happy and smiling because I was confident. I knew what I was about to do to this guy, and he's in my face very angry. I didn't understand at that time that it was the happy emotion and mood that I was in that was going to help me drop him.

Dillman illustrating how good stances
help the overall techniques.

▶ You say that, "The next generation will always be better than the past one. At least that should be the goal of every good teacher. The student should always be better than and surpass the instructor," does this still holds true?

Oh, yes, they have to, to keep this alive. At one point I was worried about something happening to me. I opened up a secret on the martial arts, and I was worried about something happening to me and no one seeing this. No one knowing about it. So I started teaching it, thinking if I can just get a few people taught to pass this on. Well now there are thousands all over the world. I can name countries around the world that are all doing pressure point techniques… We went through a period when people were dropping katas and forms, and that was based on a statement that Bruce Lee made, that I asked Bruce about personally before he died. He didn't mean it the way they were writing it. Bruce Lee said that he did not need katas and forms anymore to fight… Everyone looked at that as he didn't need them… He said, "Kata and form is you learning how to print the alphabet. You learning how to write. If you want to write somebody a letter right now, you don't print anymore. I think I could stop doing my katas and forms and fight the same, now." He didn't mean don't do them at all.

▶ How will your fighting system continue in the future?

Proper breathing and the use of sound
are part of martial art training.

I want to do a story about that... Remy Presas had a story in *Black Belt* magazine several years ago of who should take over if anything happened to him. We're working with *Black Belt* now on doing that story, and putting in everyone's picture. But I have a lot of young people that are trained really well, and I know they'll carry the ball, people like Bill Burch, Dr. Chas Terry —he's a medical doctor and an acupuncturist—Ed Lake who went on to acupuncture school, and probably knows more about pressure points than anyone in the system, because he's trained as a doctor and he's trained as a herb person. Dusty Seal is a young man with a tremendous amount of knowledge... the man that helps me write the books, Chris Thomas... I communicate with him daily. He is also a minister... so we communicate on various aspects of self-defense as well as the meaning of all this, tracing it back.

▶ WHAT WOULD YOU WANT FUTURE GENERATIONS TO REMEMBER AND YOUR INFLUENCE IN THE MARTIAL ARTS?

The fact that I made a major change in the martial arts, at least outside of the closed section of the Orient... There are people that are even using my theory that don't understand it well, but they're at least thinking about their forms, their katas, and they're trying to come up with better moves. So I think I've made a major change that I'm happy with, and I think it's going to continue for the rest of time now. If I die tomorrow, I think it's going to continue, because there's too many thousands of people that know and are teaching this theory. There are several things that they're going to have to do and develop and find out on their own, that maybe I didn't teach them if they weren't at the right place at the right time, but they should be able to develop and figure it out. I gave them the pattern to do it. I gave them the roadmap.

The passing on of martial tradition continues through generations. Here, Dillman is photographed with students who are being promoted with certificates in his system.

chapter 5

The Stories of Meibukan Goju-ryu Karate as Told by Yagi Meitatsu

by Robert Toth

Yagi Meitatsu demonstrating kata in memory of his father. Date: March 2006.

Introduction

The opportunity to spend time with the successor of the Goju style[1] of Okinawan karate is not often realized. For this author, the chance has presented itself twice. The first was in May 2004. I had invited Yagi Meitatsu to teach a seminar at our martial arts school in St. Catharines, Ontario. That afternoon, he allowed me to conduct an interview and take some pictures that were published in the *Journal of Asian Martial Arts* (Toth, 2004) as "Yagi Meitatsu discusses the not-so-secret techniques of Okinawan Gojyu-ryu karate."

Sensei Yagi was very pleased with the article. After it was published, when we'd meet for training, he'd introduce me to the attendees and ask if they had read the article. When I approached him with the idea for another article, Sensei Yagi was very much in favor of it.

STORIES

The desire to tell stories and to listen to them is inherent in the human race (Maugham, 1939: xix). Most families have stories that are passed down from generation to generation that help form their history. When Yagi Meitatsu teaches karate, he finds occasions during the class to tell stories about his father or his father's teacher, the originator of Goju-ryu, Miyagi Chojun. The stories he tells are all part of his family history and of Goju-ryu karate, as well.

On Sundays, Meitatsu's father, Meitoku, would take the family for car trips to look for antiques and visit flea markets. During these excursions, if he was in a good mood, he would regale his wife and children with stories of his teacher, Miyagi Chojun, as well as stories of Miyagi's martial arts instructors, Arakaki Ryuko and Higaonna Kanryo.

At first, Yagi Meitatsu told the stories his father had told him. But the elder Yagi would never tell of his own exploits. So, Yagi Meitatsu also shared stories he knew about his father. These are also part of Goju-ryu karate's history.

The stories of the lives of former generations are examples to the people of the modern day (Burton, n.d.: 1). In the martial arts, stories are told to educate, instruct, and entertain. Being a part of the martial arts is being involved with a history that stretches back countless millennium. The stories of the past masters help keep us connected to that stream of history that martial artists are all a part of.

The Yagi family. Meitatsu is the oldest boy sitting next to his sister.

A Short History of Goju-Ryu Karate

Miyagi Chojun started his martial arts training with Arakaki Ryuko (Sells, 2000: 81). Yagi Meitatsu tells the story of Miyagi's first meeting with Arakaki:

> One day, a tough guy was fighting in the street with many people. He was so strong that nobody could touch him. The authorities were called and two policemen came, but they couldn't control the tough either. He was just too strong. The young Miyagi Chojun stood watching. Finally, one fellow was able to get the tough guy down and hold him easily. Miyagi was amazed and he followed the man to his house and asked him to teach him. This was Miyagi's first teacher, Arakaki Ryuko.
>
> In Arakaki's small house, there was striking post [*makiwara*], stones used for weightlifting [*chishi*], earthen training jars [*nigirigame*], and all kinds of training items. Arakaki's martial art was about conditioning the body first. So, this is how Miyagi Chojun started his martial arts training. When Arakaki recognized Miyagi's talent, he introduced him to Higaonna Kanryo.

Higaonna is remembered as the man who popularized the Fujian martial arts in late 19th-century Okinawa (Sells, 2000: 45, 47). The following story about Higaonna was told to Yagi Meitatsu by his father:

> Higaonna had arranged passage on a ship to Fujian, China, to continue his martial arts training. He knew a man who was captain of a ship and he asked him to take him. Higaonna went to Fujian Province, and started training in the martial arts with Ryoto, a bamboo craftsman. After he studied for about two years, Ryoto found that Higaonna Kanryo had a talent for the marital arts. So, he introduced him to Ko Ryuru. That's the martial arts way. Higaonna trained hard and became the assistant instructor to Ko Ryuru in China. Higaonna Kanryo stayed at Ko Ryuru's house. Higaonna would sleep on the first floor and Ko Ryuru slept on the second floor. Higaonna had a bamboo bed with a thin blanket. That way he wouldn't sleep easily and he'd wake up quickly, like an animal, and when people would come he would hear them. Higaonna stayed at Ko Ryuru's house for seven or eight years.
>
> After eight years, Higaonna Kanryo went back to Okinawa. But before he left China, Ko Ryuru told him, "Don't teach the martial arts too easily." When Higaonna Kanryo returned to Okinawa, he didn't teach for almost twenty years. In that way, he kept his word to his teacher.

People in Naha recognized that Higaonna was a great martial artist and many famous people wanted him to teach. Finally, after twenty years, he began to take students. Among them were master Miyagi Chojun, Kyoda Juhatsu,[2] and Shiroma Masahige.[3]

Miyagi Chojun trained with Higaonna Kanryo until Hiagaonna's death in 1915. Afterwards, Miyagi made at least two trips to China to further his knowledge of the martial arts. He then set about perfecting the Naha-te he had inherited from Higaonna (Sells, 2000: 45, 47, 82). As a small boy, Yagi Meitatsu remembers meeting Miyagi Chojun. These are stories about Miyagi Chojun told to Meitatsu by his father:

> There are no fighting stories about Miyagi Chojun. In fact, for most of the masters there are no fighting stories.
>
> One time, Miyagi Chojun was attacked by three toughs. Miyagi curled himself into a ball to protect himself. Although the three men punched at him, they couldn't hurt him because he had developed his body to such a high degree. Miyagi covered his face with his hands, watched and waited for one of the men to kick him. When this happened, Miyagi caught the man's foot and threw him to the ground. The other two ran away.

Left: Miyagi Chojun (left) with Kyoda Juhatsu. Right: Miyagi Chojun teaching after Word War II. The period can be determined by the U.S. Army issue pants worm by students.

Miyagi was very strong. When he squeezed raw beef it would come out between his fingers like hamburger. He could crush young bamboo. The technique he used is something that has to be trained. It's all finger power. The thumb is not used.

When Miyagi Chojun was young, about twenty-five years old, a tough guy came from mainland Japan to do demonstrations. The man's manager would offer a bet that would pay back ten times if anyone could knock the tough guy down. There were some martial artists that paid the fee, punched the man but couldn't knock him down.

When he was younger, Miyagi's name was Machu. Someone asked him, "Machu, can you do it?" Miyagi replied, "Maybe." So, he paid the fee to the tough guy's manager. Miyagi stood in front of the man, punched him and the fellow fell down. The tough guy complained, "Why did you punch? I wasn't prepared." With the other martial artists, they would wait for the tough guy to be ready before they punched him, but Miyagi didn't wait. He punched him before he could prepare. This just shows how smart Miyagi was. He was a very smart young man.

• • •

When Miyagi Chojun was teaching he didn't have a dojo. He taught in his backyard. He would tell the students, "Move that stone over there. Relocate that plant over there." After two hours he'd say, "OK. You must be tired. You can go home." The next week he'd have them move the stones and plants again, but to different locations. Some of the students got tired of it. They thought that Miyagi wasn't teaching anything, so they went to another dojo where the teacher taught forms [kata]. After a few months, there were only two or three students left with Miyagi and only then did Miyagi start to teach.

There were two reasons he did this. First, Miyagi was watching the personality of each student. Second, in the Goju system, it's important to make the body strong first. Remember, Ko Ryuru didn't want Higaonna to make learning the martial arts too easy and Higaonna had passed that on to Miyagi.

• • •

Miyagi Chojun was a very severe instructor. When a student came with a towel wrapped around his neck to the dojo, he was told not to come again. When another student came to the dojo whistling, he was told not to come back. Miyagi said, "If you'd show disrespect like that to my face, what would you do behind my back?" Miyagi was very severe.

• • •

Miyagi Chojun with a group of students. Yagi Meitoku is in the middle of the back row.

• • •

A long time ago the Butokukai[4] invited Miyagi Chojun to demonstrate in Tokyo. Miyagi couldn't go. To be frank, he got sea sick when he traveled by boat. So, he sent his senior student, Shinzato Jinan.[5] At that time, in Japan, they had many different kinds of jujutsu[6] and kenjutsu.[6] After the demonstration in the changing room, some of the Japanese martial artists came to Shinzato and said, "We have names for the different styles of our martial arts. What is the name of your style?"

At that time in Okinawa, the art was just called *te* or *tode* to represent "Chinese Hand." So, when Shinzato returned to Okinawa, he reported this story to Miyagi Chojun. Now, Miyagi's family was rather well off and he knew of the old Chinese martial arts manual called the *Bubishi*.[8] Higaonna Kanryo also used to tell Miyagi about the Kempo Haiku ["Fist Way Eight Poems"] that is in the *Bubishi*. The two words Miyagi liked the most from the Kempo Haiku was "*go jyu*."

• • •

Miyagi had two favorite philosophies. The first was: to study the martial arts, you have to train in spiritual training before physical techniques. Even if you have good techniques, if you don't have a good heart, people won't follow you. The second was about how there is no competition for flowing water. It will just naturally go from up to down and someday, it will reach the sea. These are Miyagi Chojun's favorite philosophical concepts.

• • •

Left: "Fist Methods—Eight Poems" from the *Bubishi*. Right: Yagi Meitoku, Yamaguchi Gogen, and Ken Miyagi at Miyagi Chojun's grave.

Goju-ryu was the first Okinawan karate style to be named (Yagi, 2006). In 1933, Miyagi's style was formally registered as "Gojyu-Ryu" with the Butokukai (Higaonna, 1985: 28).

Yagi Meitoku was born on March 6, 1912 in Naha, Okinawa. His grandfather took him to Miyagi Chojun when he was thirteen years old (Yagi e-mail, 2004). In the early days, they taught only three katas: *Sanchin*, *Seiunchin*, and *Seisan*. Only the successor of the style would be taught all of the other katas. Miyagi taught Yagi Meitoku all of the katas (Yagi, 2006).

After Miyagi's death in 1953, the Miyagi family chose Yagi Meitoku to carry on the Goju-ryu karate system. At that time, he was given Miyagi Chojun's uniform and belt as symbols of his inheritance (Babladelis, 1992: 40). Yagi named his school *Meibukan* ("House of the Pure Warrior"; Yagi, Wheeler, and Vickerson, 1998: 49). Meitatsu started training with his father at the age of five and trained with him for over fifty years (Yagi, interview 2004). These are some of the stories Yagi Meitatsu told about his father:

> Yagi Meitoku had a very strong punch. It was strong enough to break a makiwara. I remember when I was small my father would put a makiwara near a wall with a small string between the makiwara and the wall. My father would punch the makiwara and it would move a little closer to the string. After two or three months the makiwara would touch the string and he'd move the string farther away. He'd move it again and again.

• • •

Left: Miyagi Chojun's uniform and belt.
Right: Eighteen year old Yagi Meitoku in uniform.

If someone had a new makiwara in Naha, Meitoku would often ask, "Can I try your makiwara?" They'd say, "Sure." But they wouldn't expect Yagi to be able to break it. Yagi Meitoku would punch the makiwara, and boom! He'd break it. So, later on people would say to each other, "If you build a new makiwara, don't tell Meitoku or he'll come and try it out and break it."

Later, when we would test our black belts, we'd have a makiwara test. In our style, we don't have any free fighting; only kata. So, after the student would demonstrate kata, they'd have to punch the makiwara. If they were not strong enough … well, maybe next time.

• • •

When Yagi Meitoku was in the Japanese military, he was in a group that had to take care of the horses. At that time, if a horse would bite, he'd have a red ribbon tied on top of its mane. If a horse kicked with its front legs, he would have a yellow ribbon on its neck. A horse that kicked with its rear legs, he would have a blue ribbon tied to its tail. One time there was a horse that had three ribbons because he bit and kicked with both its front and rear legs. Nobody wanted to look after it. So, the officer in charge said, "Yagi, you take care of it." So, Yagi did. Usually there was no problem.

Then one day, Yagi went to the barn and the horse was uneasy and he tried to push Yagi into a corner so he could bite him. Yagi avoided the horse. A few days later, Yagi went back to the barn. The horse was tied up, so it couldn't escape. Yagi held the horse's rope and hit the side of its face many times with his fist. The side of the horse's face was very smooth like a makiwara, and Yagi could break a makiwara.

So, he punched the horse many times. Finally, the horse fell down. Just at that moment, two or three soldiers were walking by and saw what happened. At least they saw Yagi punch the horse and the horse fall. The next day they told everyone, "Don't fight with Yagi. With one punch, he knocked down a horse!

At that time in the Japanese Army when someone made a mistake, the officer in charge would slap everybody in the unit one by one. One day there had been a mistake made in Yagi's group and the officer came to punish them. This was after the horse incident. Yagi was standing third in line. The officer came up to the first man and slapped him, then the second man and slapped him. He skipped Yagi Meitoku, then slapped the fourth man. Maybe he had it in his mind that Yagi would block and hit him back. This story was told by a classmate of Yagi Meitoku's and not by Yagi himself.

Above: Yagi Meitoku working with a makiwara in the garden dojo in the mid-1980s. Below: Yagi Meitoku was ranked in judo while he served as the chief customs officer for Naha city. He is seen here teaching judo.

Left: Demonstrating the Seipai kata in Tokyo in the early 1970s.

Left to right: Kobudo master Matayoshi Shinpo (1922-1997),
Yagi, and Toguchi Seikichi (1917-1998).

Yagi Meitoku

Yagi Meitoku in a pose from the Sanseiru
kata (left) and Kururunfa kata (right).

• • •

Yagi Meitoku chose his oldest son, Meitatsu, to be the first to learn all facets of Meibukan Goju-ryu (IMGKA, 2004). Yagi Meitatsu was born in Kume, Naha City, on July 7, 1944. At the age of five, Meitatsu started karate training with his father. They trained in their backyard six days a week for two hours a day (Yagi, interview 2004). Meitatsu tells these stories of training with his father:

> We used to practice six days a week, Monday through Saturday. We'd do apparatus training [*hojo undo*], chishi, kame, and forearm training [*kote kitae*]. The kote kitae was not just with one partner. We'd change partners over and over again. Then we'd do Sanchin. Everyday we'd do this and our arms were always bruised with no time to heal. After practice, we'd go and buy ice in a bucket to drink. This kind of training made a strong body, but when I'd go to school my hands would shake so much I had trouble holding a pencil.

• • •

Yagi's students were taught to clean up the dojo before class and not afterward. That way the teacher could see the most serious students were the ones that showed up early to do the cleaning. The others would just show up in time for class.

When they were young, Meitatsu and his fellow students would bring water for the teacher during a break. They'd also turn the teacher's sandals at the door to point toward the exit, so it would be easier for the teacher to slip them on and be on his way.

• • •

During winter training [*kangeiko*], there was no heater in the school. During the last two weeks of December, we'd practice from 4:00 to 6:00 am. At first, many people came to train, but it was too early and because it was December they were too busy so, after a week, only two showed up. Yagi Meitoku did this as spiritual or mental training.

> People have asked if my father trained my brother and I special. We were the same and equal to other people, but we always had to work harder than everyone else. I remember the senior students would chase after me with a stick to make me move faster. Every day we'd run barefoot for about twenty minutes. When I was small, I used to hate my father. Every day we had to practice, six days a week. Every New Year there would be a number of famous performers on television, but I had to miss the show. There was no video then. So, when you missed the show, that's it. But today I appreciate what my father did.

Yagi Meitatsu in a pose from the Seisan kata.

• • •

Our "two-years practice" [*ninen geiko*] was 11:00 pm December 31st to 1:00 am January 1st. The last hour of the year and the first hour of the New Year we would practice. So, the last hour of this year and the first hour of the next year you finish with karate and start with karate. You don't see your family or your girlfriend—you see your teacher and your karate group. From 11:55 to 12:05, the last five minutes of this year and the first five minutes of the New Year, we would meditate. The last five minutes of this year, you think back to what happened in the year. The first five minutes of the New Year, you make decisions or goals for the New Year. Those ten minutes are very important. Then, after the one hour training in the New Year, we would all run to the Naminoue Shrine[9] to pray. Judo and kendo students, also in their uniforms [*dogi*] would be there, too. But now it's very crowded, so we don't go anymore.

• • •

Sometimes people ask me if I like karate. I still don't know. My father made me practice. I had no choice. I believe that people don't choose a profession. The profession chooses people. The first son has an obligation that must be fulfilled. I was never told this, but I felt the responsibility. I started my sons in karate training when they were three years old. Now they are 28 and 29. They're teaching while I'm away.

When asked if he thought his oldest son would carry on after he retired, Meitatsu answered, "I hope so."

TECHNICAL SECTION — FOREARM TRAINING

Kote kitae means forearm training. In Goju-ryu karate, the body must be trained first. *Kote kitae* conditions the forearms to make them capable of delivering strong blocks and punches. The *kote kitae* drill was taught by Miyagi Chojun to Yagi Meitoku and passed on to his son Meitatsu when he was a boy. As a boy, Meitatsu would train with his father's much older and larger students. When performing the *kote kitae*, some of the senior students would be soft with him, but others would hit hard. Partners would be changed over and over again.

There is a hidden technique within the *kote kitae* drill. As the arm comes up to strike the partner's arm, it simulates poking to the eyes. Eyes cannot be hit with an up to down attack as other strikes are delivered in Goju-ryu, but they can be struck from below.

FOREARM TRAINING

1-2) Right arm middle block and low block. 3-4) Left arm middle block and low block. 5-6) Both people step forward with the right foot while performing a middle block and low block.

7-8) Both turn and face each other with left foot in front, while performing a middle block and low block. 9-10) Step back with left foot and continue with middle block and low block. 11-12) Left arm middle block and low block.

13-14) Both step forward with the right foot, while performing a middle block and low block.

15-16) Both persons turn and face each other with left foot in front while performing a middle block and low block. 17) Back to the beginning and repeat ad infinitum.

Left: Meitatsu and his wife Noriko at
Montebello Park in St. Catharines, Ontario, Canada.
Right: The author with Yagi Meitatsu in Brantford, Ontario, Canada.

Conclusion

The stories of the Yagi family make up the history of Goju-ryu karate. Whether they are anecdotes about Miyagi Chojun and his teachers or the reminiscing about Yagi Meitoku by his son, they are all a part of the greater legend of the martial arts. Another volume of stories is in the making as Yagi Meitatsu continues his obligation to his father by spreading Goju-ryu karate around the world. The Okinawan karate master meeting new people and teaching his family art in the United States, Canada, Poland, England, and other countries guarantees a new batch of stories that will be passed on to the next generation.

Notes

[1] *Goju* translates as "hard and soft." The normal spelling "*goju*" leads the non-Japanese speaker to pronounce the term harsher and give it the meaning of "fifty." Yagi Meitoku pointed this out to Ken Trebilcock during a 1995 trip to Okinawa. Yagi Meitatsu likes to use the spelling "*gojyu*" with the softer sound of "*jyu*" because it offers a more correct phonetic rendering of the term (Trebilcock, 2006).

² Kyoda Juhatsu (1887-1968) founded the style called To'on-ryu (McKenna, 2000: 33).
³ Shiroma Masahige (1890-1954) was also known as Gusukuma Shinpan. He was one of the most talented karate teachers to outlive the war. His peers considered him a brilliant technician. Unfortunately, he is also one of the least known of the old Okinawan masters. He is most remembered as a Shorin-ryu stylist, but had also trained in Naha-te (Sells, 2000: 146, 176).
⁴ The *Butokukai* (Martial Virtues Society) was founded during the Meiji period (1868-1912). The Japanese Government authorized it to research, preserve, and promote Japanese martial arts (McCarthy, 1999: 73, 74).
⁵ Until his death during World War II, Shinzato was Miyagi's senior student (Sells, 2000: 105).
⁶ *Jujutsu* ("gentle art") is a Japanese method of unarmed combat that uses the human body as a weapon.
⁷ *Kenjutsu* ("sword art") is the traditional, aggressive method of swordsmanship practiced by Japanese feudal warriors.
⁸ *Bubishi* means "to provide military ambition." It is an anthology of the history, philosophy, and application of Chinese gongfu. It is presumed that the *Bubishi* was brought from Fuzhou, Fujian, China, to Okinawa sometime during the mid-to-late-19th century (McCarthy, 1995: 12, 13, 14).
⁹ The Shinto shrine at Naminoue overlooks Naha harbor (Kerr, 2000: 415, 452).

Bibliography

Babladelis, P. (1992, December). The sensei who received Chojun Miyagi's belt. *Black Belt*.

Burton, R. (n.d.). *The Arabian nights*. New York: The Book League of America.

Farkas, E., and Corcoran, J. (1983). *The Overlook martial arts dictionary*. New York: Overlook Press.

Higaonna, M. (1985). *Traditional karate do Okinawa Goju ryu, Volume 1*. Tokyo: Minato Research Publications.

Higaonna, M. (1995). *The history of karate*. Thousand Oaks, CA: Dragon Books.

IMGKA (2004). International Meibukan Gojyu-ryu Karate Association website www.imgka.com

Kerr, G. (2000). *Okinawa – The history of an island people*. Boston: Tuttle Publishing.

Maugham, W. (1939). *The teller of tales*. New York: Doubleday, Doran and Company.

McCarthy, P. (1995, summer). The search for the *Bubishi*. *Budo Dojo*

Magazine, 12-14.

McCarthy, P. (1999). *Ancient Okinawan martial arts, Volume 2.* Boston: Tuttle Publishing.

McKenna, M. (2000). To'on-ryu–A glimpse into karate-do's roots. *Journal of Asian Martial Arts,* 9(3): 32-43.

Ricci, B. (2006, September 18). Personal communication.

Sells, J. (2000). *Unante: The secrets of karate.* Hollywood, CA: W.M. Hawley.

Toth, R. (2004). Yagi Meitatsu discusses the not-so-secret techniques of Okinawan Gojyu-Ryu karate. *Journal of Asian Martial Arts,* 13(4), 60-71.

Trebilcock, K. (2006, December 6). Personal communication.

Yagi, Mietatsu (2004, April 16). E-mail communication.

Yagi, Mietatsu (2004, May 14). Interview held in St. Catharines, Ontario, Canada.

Yagi, Mietatsu (2006, May 1). Interview held in St. Catharines, Ontario, Canada

Yagi, Mietatsu (2006, October 21). Interview held in Brantford, Ontario, Canada

Yagi, M., Wheeler, C., and Vickerson, B. (1998). *Okinawan karate-do Goju-ryu Meibu-kan.* Dundas, Ontario, Canada: self published.

Acknowledgment

The author would like to thank Sensei Yagi Meitatsu for providing the pictures of his family and of Miyagi Chojun. All of the other photos were taken by the author. Thank you, as well, to Ken Trebilcock for appearing in the photos in the technical section and for his help.

chapter 6

Politics and Karate:
Historical Influences on the Practice of Goju-ryu

by Giles Hopkins, M.A.

Illustration courtesy of iStock.com
All photographs courtesy of Giles Hopkins, except where noted.

Introduction

A few years ago, I happened on a translation of the minutes of the 1936 meeting of karate masters, government officials, and journalists in Patrick McCarthy's *Ancient Okinawan Martial Arts: Koryu Uchinadi*. The meeting was sponsored by the Ryukyu Newspaper Company, but its primary organizer was Nakasone Genwa (1886-1978). Though Mr. Nakasone went on to publish a number of books on karate (*Karate no Kenkyu*, 1934; *Karate-do Taikan*, 1938; *Kobo Kenpo Karatedo Nyumon*, 1938, with Mabuni Kenwa), he seemed a curious figure to be so instrumental in this gathering of prominent martial artists. McCarthy notes that after graduating from college, Nakasone moved to Tokyo, became involved in the socialist movement there, and "served as the publisher of its newspaper" (1999: 58). It struck me then that this ancient tradition of martial arts—a tradition, it has been suggested, going back to Bodhidharma—was not immune to the pressures of politics and different social agendas. Perhaps I was naïve to think there was anything that could survive the insidious influence of politics.

As I closed the book, I thought about my impressions of Okinawa. I could hear crickets in the distance. Dogs were barking and it was hot and humid.

It was hot there too. In Okinawa, we slept on *tatami* mats in a small apartment that Matayoshi Shinpo sensei (1922-1997) had given us for the summer, just above the vegetable market—my teacher, me, and one other student. Trucks from the countryside began their deliveries at three or four in the morning. Awakened by the dogs and the constant jockeying of delivery vans through the small streets, we were tired by mid-day. The soft tar in the road yielded under the weight of each step. Sweat dripped down the center of our backs, soaking our shirts. June bugs screeched like cats held at bay when small boys trapped them with butterfly nets and stowed them safely in cages tied to their belts.

We were usually up soon after sunrise, setting off in search of coffee through the seemingly endless market stalls of Heiwa Dori (Peace Street)—a maze of intersecting covered alleyways, restricted to pedestrian traffic, that began after World War II as a marketplace run by the widows of Okinawan soldiers. In the aftermath of the war, wing sections of downed fighter planes were dismantled and used for shelters, many of them making up the walls and roofs of the original market. Now, of course, it's all very modern; Naha, the capital of Okinawa, is mostly concrete and glass.

But not far from the office buildings and department stores that crowd the center of Naha, one can still see wooden houses with sliding doors and tile roofs that survived the devastation of the war. Walking through the narrow streets, where potters have continued to make the old jars that karate students (*karateka*) call gripping jars (*nigirigame*), one can still experience glimpses of an Okinawa that has all but disappeared. The signs are still there, pointing the way to an old craftsman who still makes the traditional Okinawan weapons or to a small training hall (*dojo*) tucked away at the end of a narrow alley. Most of the young people in Okinawa are playing baseball on hard-packed dirt fields. But a few still find their way to the dojo, their shoes lined up just inside the door. The cadences of training can be heard from the street. Though many things have changed, Okinawa has managed to survive the terrible events of the 20th century. But the gnawing question remained—at what cost?

Sitting in my kitchen that evening, thinking about McCarthy's book, I sensed that Okinawan karate may also have been under attack in the first half of the 20th century—even before the Second World War—and it was an attack that seemed to be far more subtle, and yet, for that very reason, potentially far more significant for the martial arts.

Above: The author with gripping jars (*nigirigame*) and an old pottery shop where they are made. Below: The interior of an old style house. Turning a grindstone with the help of ox power.

An old style house in the midst of Naha city which managed to survive WW II.

The Realities of History

Many of us still naively believe that traditions—or the high-mindedness of certain larger-than-life individuals—may protect a practice from the social or political influences of the world in which it exists. In some circles, there is the rather ingenuous notion that traditional arts are somehow independent of politics. But everything is political in one sense or another.

To suggest that any martial art, traditional or otherwise, can develop in a political vacuum is to say that it exists outside of history. This is the same as arguing that Shakespeare or Mozart or Picasso are somehow independent of the historical events that in fact shaped them. We are tempted to imagine that their work exists outside history because it seems transcendent—that is, it resonates today as much as it did with generations of sympathetic students of the arts in the past—but it is just not the case.

In the martial arts, we have ritual and tradition, both serving to preserve our practice and connect us to the past in a way that would also seem to transcend historical evolution. It is an inescapable irony that in practicing traditional karate—an admittedly anachronistic pastime—we wish to connect with some evanescent past, shrouded in the mists of legend, while at the same time disavowing any connection with modern history, in this case the influences of the 20th century.

As students of history, however, we must try to understand these historical influences in order to understand what we practice today. How can we separate what is truly traditional from what is merely expedient, the essential from what has been grafted on to it out of political necessity?

The underlying agenda of the 1936 Ryukyu Newspaper Company meeting—etched in fine print between the lines of text—was to find ways to popularize karate, make it more acceptable to the public, and give it a less violent image. In the process, there was a not-so-subtle attempt to make karate less Chinese, to Japan-ize karate. Were there underlying political reasons for this push to change and popularize karate?

Japanese Politics in the Early Years of the 20th Century

In 1936, Japan was awash with fear and domestic terrorism. The previous decade in Japanese politics saw a "resurgence of right-wing patriotism, the weakening of democratic forces, domestic terrorist violence (including an assassination attempt on the emperor in 1932), and stepped-up military aggression abroad" (Library of Congress, "The Rise of the Militarists," hereafter, LOC Militarists). Japan had already withdrawn from the League of Nations and military leaders were looking for any excuse to strengthen their hold on Manchuria "as an industrial base, an area for Japanese emigration, and a staging ground for war with the Soviet Union" (LOC Militarists).

Hirohito had taken the throne in 1927 and nationalist groups were calling for a return to traditional Japanese values—"the ideals of ... self-sacrifice in service of the nation"—to the "exclusion of Western influences" (LOC Militarists). Since the first Sino-Japanese War of 1894-95, Japanese military leaders were embarking on more and more provocative actions in Manchuria and attempting to exert more control in Japanese governmental affairs "aimed at setting up a national socialist state" (LOC Militarists). Even European nations and the United States were seen as a threat since the last decade of the 19th century—and unquestionably in the aftermath of the 1900 Boxer Rebellion—interested in dividing China into various "spheres of interest," a policy they euphemistically referred to as "carving up the Chinese melon" (Hooker, 1996). Though Japan appeared to be as hegemonic as any European power in the decades that followed, one can certainly understand the rise in militaristic nationalism to protect their regional interests. But perhaps the motivation of Japan's military leaders was prompted by nothing more than an age-old animosity between China and Japan. Was this the divine retribution to be visited on China in response to the invasions of Kublai Khan so many centuries before?

In any event, this rekindling of patriotic zeal coupled with an anti-

Chinese bias is evident in the minutes of the 1936 meeting, and it had two quite important effects on the martial arts: The first was the push to popularize karate and develop a curriculum that could be safely taught in schools, a sort of quasi-martial training to indoctrinate the youth. In order to do this, the public perception of karate would need to be changed from a brutal form of hand-to-hand combat to one of physical education. In fact, if one could emphasize spiritual as well as physical development, it would be even better. The second effect would be to separate karate from its Chinese roots; change its name; and make new, Japanese forms (*kata*).

The Situation in Okinawa

In his short essay *An Outline of Karatedo*, which McCarthy dates March 23, 1934, it is evident Miyagi Chojun was already thinking about the nature of karate and its popular perception by the time of the 1936 meeting. In this early essay, Miyagi emphasized that "training in karate-do improves one's health" and that "physical and mental unity develops an indomitable spirit" (McCarthy, 1999: 51). Certainly, these were laudable goals and might even convince a wary public that the aim of true karate practice was in keeping with traditional Japanese values and would develop physical as well as spiritual strength in Japan's youth. Though at times in the minutes of the 1936 masters meeting, it would seem that there were disagreements—most notably over the place and importance of classical (of Chinese origin) katas—it is clear that the participants were generally united in their efforts to popularize Okinawan karate.

Some have suggested that the impetus for this move may have had more expedient financial motivations behind it. The post-war depression of the 1920's hit Okinawa perhaps harder than other parts of Japan. Broadening karate's appeal would benefit karate instructors financially at a time when most Okinawans were not very well off. George Kerr sums it up succinctly, if somewhat dryly, when he states that "Okinawa suffered extreme hardship; the prefecture was at the bottom of the list in the distribution of aid on a national scale" (1958: 434). On average, the standard of living seemed to be increasing in the first two decades of the 20th century, but Okinawa's economy was still "last and least in comparison with the advances which had been made in other prefectures of Japan" (Kerr, 1958: 434). Why the disparity?

Okinawa itself exerted little influence over its own affairs as a young prefecture and certainly less over Japanese national interests, having "only five representatives in a Lower House membership of 381" (Kerr, 1958: 428). As early as the first Sino-Japanese War, "Official [Japanese] policy stiffened and remained hostile thereafter to all local traditions and folkways which marked off Okinawans from other loyal subjects in the empire" (1958: 422). Prejudice towards these poor country cousins more often than not seemed to dictate policy. As Kerr points out, the Okinawans had almost no influence in the "matter of appointments to the governorship" (1958: 429) and, by 1919, Okinawa "showed increasing export deficits" (1958: 432).

The island's economy gradually came under the control of the central government and Japanese industry, yet the Japanese Government seemed to offer little in the way of aid or reform. So much so, Kerr suggests, that it seemed as if "'Economic colonization' had replaced 'political colonization'" (1958: 432). To cope with a poor economic outlook and an increasing population, the government encouraged emigration. As callous as this "solution" seems to be, "By 1930, more than 54,000 had left Okinawa for foreign lands" (Kerr, 1958: 438), sending money home, aiding development, and adding a source of revenue that was not dependent on the national coffers, exactly what the government had been hoping for.

The second step the central government took to address economic problems had the two-fold benefit of not only defraying the cost of local governmental services, but also ensuring a sort of civic-mindedness in Okinawan citizens. The government encouraged participation in any number of local associations. Membership was supposedly voluntary but, as George Kerr points out, "everyone in a community was expected to belong to one or more of the associations" (1958: 429). The associations made "contributions of time, labor, material, or money" to provide for "the costs of fire fighting, road repair, maintenance of shrine grounds and parks, work on public buildings" and the like (Kerr, 1958: 429).

In addition to economic difficulties, the first quarter of the 20th century also saw an Okinawan crisis in health and healthcare. This was not surprising given the economic hardships the Okinawans faced, but there was also a shortage of doctors. The Ryukyu Islands were not an attractive location after one had spent years studying to become a doctor—no one was going to get rich in Okinawa. "Okinawa Prefecture had the lowest recorded venereal disease rate" in Japan in 1905, but 25 years later Okinawa "had the highest rates in the country for both venereal disease and tuberculosis" (1958: 440). Because Japan was preparing for war in the 1930's, "there was a quickening interest in national health standards and public welfare" (Kerr, 1958: 440)—certainly something a number of karate teachers must have been aware of when they noted the health benefits of karate training in their writings.

The Japanization Program

Though Japan may have been reluctant to address economic and political problems—that is, to offer any sound economic solutions or provide any significant political autonomy—in Okinawa, it did not seem slow in recognizing the need to assimilate the erstwhile Kingdom of the Ryukyus. This was the real goal, and "the educational system took the lead in the 'Japanization' program" (Kerr, 1958: 447). Where "speech, dress, and food habits set the Okinawans somewhat apart" (Kerr, 1958: 454), education was a means to minimize if not completely erase these differences.

The number of schools increased dramatically in the first thirty years of the 20th century and so did the number of matriculating students. Education, it might be argued, was at least a long-term means for improving the economic outlook of Okinawa, but it also served the more immediate purpose of indoctrination, creating a sense of national identity.

A growing sense of national pride seemed to accompany the defeat of China in 1895 and no doubt helped to bolster the central government's efforts to assimilate the younger generation of Okinawans. According to Kerr, "the traditions and history of old Ryukyu meant little to them" and "Chinese learning withered away with the older generation" (1958: 445). Kerr suggests that it also "quickened a desire to be considered 'up-to-date' at Naha and Shuri, and to abandon old-fashioned customs" (1958: 442). The younger generation in particular took up "the changing fashions" and even went so far as to take "distinctly Japanese names" (Kerr, 1958: 442).

Sports, particularly the Japanese sports of kendo and judo, were central to this effort to bring the once independent Ryukyu Kingdom under the banner of the Japanese Empire. Exercise and athletics not only satisfied a need to address recent health concerns in Okinawa, but also "played an important part in Japan's assimilation program," Kerr notes (1958: 446). Okinawan karate, introduced to the schools in the early years of the 20th century and fully integrated as "a part of the regular school curricula" by 1933 (McCarthy, 1999: 49), could only benefit from this association, many must have thought, particularly if it were to introduce "new" katas and terminology that would be seen as Japanese (rather than Okinawan or Chinese). It was the means to keep a tradition alive in the guise of something new. It may also have been the impetus for Okinawan karate teachers to seek recognition and grade from Japan and the Dai Nippon Butokukai, which recognized karatedo as an official style/tradition (*ryu*) in 1933 and granted Miyagi Chojun the title of *kyoshi* (All-ryu Network, "Chronology 1900-1949.").

Certainly one should acknowledge that assimilation is never as easy as it might seem in retrospect. The younger generation aside, there were others in Okinawa, foreigners included, who were very much interested in promoting and preserving Okinawa's history and traditions. A few Okinawan scholars, though trained and educated at Japanese universities, were taking an interest and writing attention-getting articles. Interest in some circles was enough to prompt the formation of an "Association for the Preservation of Historic Sites and Relics of Okinawa" (Kerr, 1958: 456). By 1930, Shuri Castle had been declared a "National Treasure" and a four-year program of restoration and repair had begun (Kerr, 1958: 456).

The walls and entry of the
reconstructed Shuri Castle.

A reconstructed Shuri Castle
~ perhaps once the symbol of the Ryukyu Kingdom.

But this interest in the past, however small it may have seemed to the general populace, "was not at all to the liking of the military men and extreme nationalist agitators at Tokyo, and led to a minor crisis in Japanese-Okinawan relations on the eve of the Pacific War" [1937-1945] (Kerr, 1958: 456)—nor was it to the liking of those in positions of power. After public outcry questioning government tactics "to suppress local peculiarities of speech and custom," according to Kerr, the governor stated "vigorously the official view that every vestige of Okinawa's provincial individuality must be erased" (1958: 457).

• • •

Admittedly, this is a brief outline of the political and economic influences at work in Okinawa in the first decades of the 20th century, but it is enough to raise questions about the direction karate took in the years and decades that followed. Did economic hardship play a significant role in the push to popularize karate? In popularizing karate, was the essence of karate watered down to the point where it was no longer a deadly martial art but merely an athletic endeavor to promote spiritual and physical well-being? Did the rise of the Japanese militarists and an aggressive foreign policy towards China cut the ties of tradition and serve merely to bolster the idea of karate as a sport—to Japan-ize what had long been referred to as "Chinese hand"?

The effort to make karate more appealing to the general public may have come from a need to offer something positive, some cultural palliative, to counter the economic hardships of the times; the island was over-crowded and economically depressed with very little political influence of its own to remedy its ills. But it also may have been politically motivated—part of an attempt to assimilate the Okinawans and remove Chinese influence.

In any event, this push toward physical fitness and an "indomitable spirit" is something that reflected the militant nationalism and aggressive foreign policy of Japan in the 1930's. It had been building steadily in the early years of the 20th century, and played out in Japan's imperialistic incursions into Manchuria and later in China proper. This was the atmosphere that informed and in some sense shrouded the 1936 masters meeting sponsored by the Ryukyu Newspaper Company. Less than a year after this meeting, the Second Sino-Japanese War began.

The 1936 Masters Meeting

The larger question for Okinawan karate, of course, is whether politics and the economic realities of the day had any significant and lasting effect on the development of karate in the 20th century. We know at least that the name changed. According to the minutes of the 1936 meeting, Nakasone Genwa's first order of business was to recommend that the name of Okinawan karate be officially changed, using the Japanese characters for "empty hand" instead of the characters for "Chinese hand," as had been the tradition. Though there seems to be no real objection to this name change, some participants at the meeting pointed out that the general population recognized the term *toudi* (the Okinawan Hogen term for Chinese hand), or more simply *te* (hand). At least in part, it seemed to be a question of familiarity, what was recognizable. Others, however, pointed out that there were those—particularly in the school systems—who "resent[ed] the term *Tou* [China]" (McCarthy, 1999: 64).

In this case, it seems fairly clear that this is a political issue—a change in tradition driven by the exigencies of contemporary politics. In fact, in view of Japan's overall assimilation program, growing animosity towards China, and disparaging view of Okinawan culture one would certainly expect this move. But, one might ask, what's in a name? As Miyagi sensei suggests: "Names change, like examples do, it depends upon the times" (McCarthy, 1999: 61), as if to imply that this would be a change in name only, having little other effect on the practice of karate or how it was taught.

Of course, less cynically, in making karate seem more Japanese, it might also make it more acceptable to the general population. Yet which changes are acceptable because they are inconsequential and which changes are unacceptable because their effect is detrimental? Certainly when we look back on the efforts of the more militant Japanese nationalists to "erase" Okinawan traditions, we are appalled and recognize how destructive such an attitude is. How then should we look at the seemingly innocuous changes suggested by politicians, military leaders, and journalists at this 1936 masters meeting?

The second order of business at the 1936 meeting, forwarded by Vice Commander Fukushima Kitsuma of the regional military headquarters, was to recommend that new katas—Japanese katas with Japanese names—be created. Behind this suggestion, coming as it does from outside the circle of Okinawan karate masters, is the need to eradicate evidence of Chinese influence on Japanese culture. Ostensibly, of course, the discussion is again couched in terms that suggest a need to popularize Okinawan karate, which, as Nakasone Genwa suggests, "is in a slump these days" (McCarthy, 1999: 65). However, in no uncertain terms, Miyagi says that "the classical kata must remain" (McCarthy, 1999: 65). In fact, he reiterates this point, underlining the importance of the Toudi katas to an understanding of the art, saying, "classical kata must remain intact, otherwise they will be forgotten" (McCarthy, 1999: 66). It is easy to understand why he was so insistent when one remembers the first precept of Goju-ryu put forward by Miyagi: secret principles exist in the Goju-ryu katas—and of course the katas he was referring to here are the classical katas of Chinese origin.

Yet even Miyagi, echoing a number of the non-martial artists at the meeting, agreed that new kata, "suitable kata … for students from elementary school to university level, should be developed" (McCarthy, 1999: 65).[1] The question for Miyagi Chojun was whether one could do both; that is, popularize karate and preserve its traditions without losing the essence of the art.

Preserving a Tradition

Miyagi was adamant about preserving the old katas—the classical subjects. But the *bunkai*—the analysis of katas or the applications of the techniques—did not need to be taught. Without knowledge of the bunkai, the kata movements merely become dance or at best an agreeable form of exercise. Karate remained intact, but it was fundamentally different—it was safe. It could be used to promote health. One would become stronger and healthier, gain confidence and polish one's spirit, but no one would get seriously hurt. Here was the means to preserve and popularize what was essentially an anachronistic and brutal pugilistic endeavor, in reality meant to kill or maim.

This might explain why Mabuni Kenwa's *Kobo Jizai Goshinjutsu Karatedo Kenpo* and a number of his other works that included discussions of katas, published in the 1930's, only show very elementary bunkai, not the katas' more deadly applications (See inset comparison). Mabuni was a close friend of Miyagi's, active in the *Ryukyu Tou-te Kenkyukai*, an association founded in 1918 to preserve the Okinawan martial arts. Mabuni also stressed the health aspect of karate training and one of its primary goals, that of "cultivating a strong, healthy body and mind" (McKenna, 2002: 13), echoing many of the same sentiments or repeating many of the same reasons that Miyagi had emphasized in his earlier *Karatedo Gaisetsu*. In fact, Mabuni quotes Ito Daisho, saying that karate training would "instill patriotism and train individuals to stand-up in times of crisis for their country …an effective form of mental training" (McKenna, 2002: 14).

There were other ways to preserve the techniques of kata and bow to the pressure to popularize karate as well, to change the public perception of karate, stressing the idea of physical and spiritual development. The Goju-ryu kata *Tensho* (revolving hands) is a case in point.

The drawings (adapted from Mabuni, 2002) and photographs show differences in interpreting applications. These attempt to illustrate the point made in the text that Mabuni may have downplayed the deadliness of karate to adapt to a political agenda.

Tensho Kata

In his *Karatedo Gaisetsu*, Miyagi Chojun refers to Tensho as a fundamental exercise (*kihon kata*), similar to Sanchin kata. With the practice of these exercises, Miyagi says, "students learn to regulate their breath while coordinating it with the use of their power in a correct posture." The purpose of kihon kata, he states, is to develop "a strong physique while encouraging a budo spirit" (Miyagi, 1934/1993: 23). The focus here is placed on posture, breath, skeletal alignment, muscular development, and so on—in a word, physical and spiritual development rather than the practice of clearly defined self-defense scenarios.

These katas differ then from the open-hand formal exercises (*kaishu kata*) that contain, as Miyagi says, "both offensive and defensive techniques in various paradigms" (Miyagi, 1934/1993: 24). In other words, kaishu kata—Saifa, Seiunchin, Shisochin, Seipai, Sanseiru, Seisan, Kururunfa, and Suparinpei—are composed of combinations that show specific applications, while the kihon kata—though they contain fundamental or basic techniques—are used to condition the body and train posture and breathing. And for anyone familiar with Goju-ryu training, there is a distinct difference in the place of kihon- and kaishu-kata in training.

An old style building
near the Shuri Castle.

The kihon kata Sanchin is taught very early, at white-belt level, and developed over the course of years of strenuous practice. The breathing is audible and the techniques, basic punches and blocks, are performed slowly with tension in sanchin stance (*dachi*). The teacher usually calls the student through the exercise and does a hands-on check for proper balance, alignment, muscular tension, and the like. It is often said that Sanchin, or "three battles," trains the mind, the body, and the spirit.

On the other hand, the kihon kata Tensho is taught at a higher level, at brown-belt or as an advanced black belt kata. Whereas the practice of Sanchin kata often begins formal class training, Tensho is often used to end training. If Sanchin is used to develop the hard aspect (*go*) of Goju-ryu, Tensho is said to develop the soft side (*ju*). Sanchin is a part of the Goju-ryu curriculum that Miyagi learned from Higashionna Kanryo and presumably one of the katas Higashionna brought from China. The history of Tensho kata, however, is a good bit murkier.

After a decade training with Higashionna, Miyagi Chojun went to China, by most accounts to visit the places his teacher had trained and meet Higashionna's teacher, Ko Ryuru. Miyagi was traveling in the company of Go Kenki (Wu Xiangui), a Chinese tea merchant living in Naha and a friend of Miyagi's, who acted as translator. Go Kenki was also a White Crane gongfu teacher (*shifu*).

There are differing opinions as to the duration of either of Miyagi's research trips to China (he would return in 1936, again in the company of Go Kenki). Were they a matter of weeks, months, or years? Was he there only long enough to observe training methods and techniques, or did he learn katas and study with a Chinese teacher? [See Ravignat, 2004, for some interesting discussion of what Miyagi may have brought back with him from China.] The question is how influential or productive these trips were for Miyagi.

There has been some recent speculation that Miyagi did not find Higashionna's teacher, who may in fact have been Wai Xianxian, not Ko Ryuru (Ravignat, 2004). Without this link, it is difficult to know what Miyagi studied in China or how much of an influence it had. Some researchers suggest that Miyagi may have developed Tensho from his study of rokkishu found in the *Bubishi* or that it is based on a Five Ancestors Fist gongfu form or perhaps a Wing Chun form (McKenna, 2006). Others have suggested that the main influence in Miyagi's development of Tensho kata was really Go Kenki, who was living on Okinawa, and who had been training with and sharing White Crane gongfu techniques with some of the great teachers in Okinawa for some time (Ravignat, 2004, part II).

In any event, what research and tradition both suggest is that Miyagi formalized the movements of Tensho kata and added it to the curriculum he had learned from Higashionna, whether it came from his research in China or his studies with Go Kenki in the Kenkyukai. What is not clear is why Miyagi felt a need to introduce these particular techniques into the Goju-ryu curriculum; that is, since there is no need to introduce something that is already there, what was missing?

The other question—apparent to anyone familiar with the training of Tensho kata in a traditional Goju-ryu dojo—is why Miyagi chose to downplay the applications of the techniques in Tensho, referring to it as a kihon kata. Used in this fashion, the emphasis, as in Sanchin kata, is on developing breathing and, for lack of a better word, internal energy (*ki*). Its soft, flowing hand movements seem more closely related to *qigong* than karate, and yet this is how it has been preserved in the traditional training regimen of Goju-ryu. Even to use it as a kind of pushing hands or arm conditioning exercise (*kakite*) as Marvin Labatte suggests (Labbate, 2001), merely reinforces the notion of using the kata as a form of physical and spiritual conditioning.

There are, however, very real self-defense applications contained within Tensho's flowing hand movements, yet they are rarely ever trained as such. Historically, the implication is that many teachers, Miyagi included, may have felt a need to de-emphasize karate's brutality in favor of its health benefits. The structure of Tensho kata and the manner in which it is generally performed both tend to hide the martial techniques and their applications. Emphasizing these aspects of Tensho may have satisfied a certain political agenda

What Was Lost

The structure of Tensho kata raises a number of interesting questions, since it is different from Goju-ryu's other classical kaishu katas. The other katas have clearly designed combinations that show quite specific application sequences, composed of entry and controlling techniques and finishing techniques (Hopkins, 2002); Tensho does not. Appearances suggest that Tensho was constructed over the basic framework of Sanchin—three steps forward and three steps back, in basic stance (*kihon dachi*), finishing with a circular block (*mawashi-uke*)—to preserve a set of basic hand techniques—techniques that showed a similarity to the established canon of Goju-ryu katas, but were different enough that they needed their own kata to preserve them intact.

If the kata techniques are rearranged into blocks and attacks—admittedly an exercise that raises red flags for some purists and certainly some questions of interpretation—one will see five blocks and five attacks covering the upper, middle, and lower target areas. They are done first with the right hand, then with the left hand, and finally with both hands (see illustrations 1a-e and 2a-e).

TECHNICAL SECTION

Tensho Kata   1a-e → blocks   2a-e → attacks

By appearance, they seem to be White Crane in nature, similar to some of the open-hand techniques of other Goju-ryu katas. It is easy to find palm strikes, knife-hand (*shuto*) attacks, and open-hand blocking in other katas. Yet this very similarity raises the question of why Miyagi saw the need to add these particular techniques to the Goju-ryu canon; that is, what is distinctive about Tensho kata?

The first and perhaps most obvious difference is that the hand techniques preserved in Tensho are executed off the front foot, unlike so many of the attacking hands in the other katas. (For example: Sanchin kata executes punches almost exclusively off the rear foot—that is, a left punch, for instance, from a right-foot-forward stance—as do Seisan, Sanseiru, and Suparinpei. See picture 3 of punch from Saifa).

Another noticeable difference is that Tensho lacks any real movement of the feet in relation to the hand techniques—that is, the hands move independent of any stepping or turning of the body. This is very different from what we generally see in the other Goju-ryu classical katas, suggesting two possible explanations: One, Tensho's hand techniques are merely that, hand techniques or basics, if you will, and they are not shown in application the same way techniques are shown in the other classical katas; or two, they are shown from a set stance position because they represent "inside" techniques, quick hand responses when the defender cannot move to the outside of the attack.

One of the fundamental principles found in the kaishu kata would suggest that the defender's first inclination in applying the techniques found in Goju-ryu katas is to move to the outside of the attack or to employ what some Chinese styles refer to as a "changing gate" method of first moving and blocking to the outside and then changing to the inside as one counterattacks. This is illustrated by the patterns and stepping inherently connected to the techniques' applications (Hopkins, 2004).

On the other hand, the techniques of Tensho kata seem to work as inside techniques, suggesting one thing that Miyagi may have thought was missing in Goju-ryu.

The other difference one notices is that the blocks and attacks are executed with the same hand, unlike the kaishu kata where the initial block and attack is generally simultaneous, blocking with one hand while attacking with the other (see picture 4 of Seipai double technique in cat stance). Together these differences suggest techniques that are meant to be used as "inside" counterattacks; that is, the opponent attacks with a left upper-level punch and the defender (using the kata's first technique) blocks with the right wing-like hand and immediately follows it with a right knife-edge (*shuto*) attack to the opponent's neck (see illustrations 5a and 5b). This is the kata's first block-and-attack sequence.

The kata's second sequence is a bit more problematic. The kata's structure obscures the technique's application, and the breathing pattern— underscored by its status as a kihon kata—does not correspond in each case with the technique; that is, inhaling on blocks and exhaling on attacks is not necessarily the rule in Tensho.[2]

As the kata is performed, the first sequence is followed by an upper-level palm strike (see 6-a). Then the hand is brought to the side (either to the hip in some schools or to the chamber position by the ribs in others) in a circular motion, followed by a lower-level palm strike, fingers pointing down (see 6-b). One can see that in the performance of the kata, Miyagi has chosen to put two attacks together, an upper-level and a lower-level palm strike. He follows these two attacks with the two blocks that are meant to accompany them: a rising wrist block (see 6-c) and a dropping wrist block (see 6-d). These blocking moves might, in fact, be more easily referred to as "painting the fence," as they are described in the 1984 *Karate Kid* movie.

In application, the opponent attacks with a left punch, either to the chest or head. The defender blocks with the rising wrist block, followed immediately with a palm strike to the face (see 7a and 7b). It is important when executing each of Tensho's blocking positions that the elbow be kept in and down.

The next application sequence shows the opponent attacking with a left punch, either to the chest or stomach. The defender blocks with the dropping wrist block, followed immediately with a palm strike to the opponent's stomach or groin (see 8-a and 8-b).

It is easy to see the simple logic and effectiveness of these techniques. But it is also easy to see that by rearranging the sequence of the techniques, the kata's structure effectively obscures any understanding of how to apply them. In addition, by emphasizing deep, rhythmical breathing and slow hand movements the focus is placed on health and conditioning more than self-defense and martial effectiveness.

The next application sequence shows the opponent attacking with a left middle-level punch. The defender blocks with a horizontal or side wrist block, followed immediately with a palm strike to the opponent's ribs (see 9-a and 9-b). Again, it is important that the elbow be kept in as the forearm is canted out. This series is performed in application the same as it is in kata.

The final block and attack sequence—if one does not include the ending *mawashi-uke* since it is certainly not unique to Tensho—is only shown in the kata as a double-hand technique stepping back. It is done three times in the kata. It shows an inside forearm block, followed by a spear-hand (*nukite*) attack. If it is executed singly against a punch, it shows the use of the fingertips in striking (see illustrations 10-a and 10-b).

Thus the kata shows methods of striking, from knife-edge to palm to fingertips, and blocking, from the wrist to the forearms in a variety of angles, all from an inside and close-in position, utilizing the same hand for both block and attack. Certainly there are disadvantages to this same-handed block and attack defense. For one, it is slower than blocking with one hand while simultaneously attacking with the other. It also requires more advanced timing. However, there are also advantages. One is that the defender's counterattacking hand is already on the inside of the opponent's guard. As the opponent senses the attack, his flinch response is to pull his own hand in to cover. Doing so, however, merely facilitates the defender's attack, helping to pull the *shuto*, in the first block and attack sequence for example, into the intended target.

While the techniques of Tensho seem straightforward enough, they are difficult to apply in reality; they require a greater degree of expertise than many of the "outside" blocking and attacking techniques of the other katas. The techniques of Tensho also demand a certain understanding of "short power"—that is, the ability to attack without chambering the hand. What is clear from this analysis, however, is that Tensho kata should also be trained with speed and power—the techniques were meant to be used. In most cases, students engaged in the practice of Tensho look as if they are painting elaborate pictures in the air or blessing the masses as if they were martial monks performing magical rites.

1936 Meeting of Karate Masters.
Photograph courtesy of Graham Noble.

Tensho will no doubt remain a kihon kata in the Goju-ryu classical kata canon, and students will continue to perform it in a slow, rhythmical fashion, focusing on breath and posture, connecting in some spiritual way with the great teachers of the past. We may never know why Miyagi chose to conceal the applications of Tensho. But we should remember that what we take for tradition was itself shaped by the necessities of another day. Like other times, politics and economics are constantly at play, and it is probable that they had a profound effect on the practice of karate and the way it was preserved. Perhaps, if we are careful, we can scrape off some of this veneer of political influence or economic expediency and get at the substance underneath it all—in this case, the essence of the art or what it might have been originally.

Conclusion

It was the end of the summer. The sounds of the market woke us for the last time. We still hadn't gotten used to it. This was not the contemplative silence of a Japan one sees in a Hiroshige print. When we arrived in Okinawa almost two months earlier, we found it to be full of surprises. It had seemed then as if Okinawa had been covered in concrete after the devastation of the Second World War. We had expected something different, but the magic and mystery of Okinawa was still there, just beneath the surface.

We often stopped to visit with Matayoshi's wife, before heading off on our explorations, just as we did this morning, our last. She offered us rice balls and we talked with her as she collected money from the small farmers or gardeners that rented space in the market to sell their produce. Her granddaughter, Nami, played in the back of the office. Some mornings Matayoshi himself would come by and haul us off to visit a famous dance teacher or we would all climb into someone's offered van and head off to see the sights of Okinawa.

But this morning we were waiting for a van to take us to the airport. To pass the time, Kimo Wall[3] was doing magic tricks for Matayoshi's granddaughter. When he held his hands out, palms up, to show her that they were empty, she looked up with surprise.

"*Doku des'ka* (Where is it)?" she asked. The coin had disappeared.

"I don't know," Kimo said, with feigned innocence. "I've forgotten where I put it. Maybe it's lost." Matayoshi laughed too. He had seen these tricks before. In a minute, the coin would appear again from behind Nami's ear or it would fall from the air as if by magic, our attention on other things.

We look to see what is hidden in the hand, but we don't see it. Sometimes I wonder what else is hidden, what else may have been lost with the deaths of so many of the old masters, lost like Nami's coin, or whether we have simply forgotten where and how to look.

Matayoshi Shinpo
with the author's daughter Emily.

Acknowledgment

A special thanks to John Jackson for help in demonstrating applications, along with my wife Martha, and our daughter Phoebe for taking the pictures.

Notes

[1] By 1940, Miyagi sensei, with Nagamine Shoshin of Shorin-ryu, had created Gekisai dai Ichi kata for use in middle schools (All Gojuryu Network, "Chronology 1900-1949").

[2] It is interesting to note that if one adheres strictly to this "rule of breath," as Labbate does in his 2001 article, one must rather awkwardly interpret the more obvious shuto attack of the first sequence as a block.

[3] Kimo Wall, 7th-dan, studied Goju-ryu under Higa Seiko and *kobudo* (ancient weapons) under Matayoshi Shinpo (1921-1997). In addition to the martial arts, he studied healing arts as well. He lives in Panajachel, Guatemala, where he teaches martial arts and Thai massage (*Nuad bo rarn*).

Bibliography

All Gojuryu Network. Chronology 1900-1949. http://www.gojuryu.net/view page.php?page_id=31

Hooker, R. (1996). Ch'ing China: The boxer rebellion. Accessed on July 10, 2006 from http://www.wsu.edu:8001/~dee/ching/boxer.htm

Hopkins, G. (2002). The lost secrets of Okinawan Goju-ryu: What the kata shows. *Journal of Asian Martial Arts, 11*(4): 54-77.

Hopkins, G. (2004). The shape of kata: The enigma of pattern. *Journal of Asian Martial Arts, 13*(1): 64-77.

Kerr, G. (1958). *Okinawa: The history of an island people*. Rutland, Vermont: Tuttle.

Labbate, M. (2001). Tensho kata: Goju-ryu's secret treasure. *Journal of Asian Martial Arts, 10*(1): 84-99.

Library of Congress. A country study: Japan. "The rise of the militarists. http://lcweb2.loc.gov/frd/cs/jptoc.html.

Library of Congress. A country study: Japan. "Two-party system." http://lcweb2.loc.gov/frd/cs/jptoc.html.

Mabuni, K. (2002). *Kobou jizai goshin-jutsu karate kenpo*. Translation and commentary by Mario McKenna. Internet publication.

McCarthy, P., and McCarthy, Y. (1999). *Ancient Okinawan martial arts: Koryu Uchinadi, Vol. 2*. Boston: Tuttle.

McKenna, M. (2006). A little more on Tensho and Rokkishu. Accessed on Aug. 4, 2006 from http://okinawakarateblog.blogspot.com

Miyagi, C. (1934/1993). *An outline of karate-doh*. Translated by Patrick and Yuriko McCarthy. Fujiwara, Japan: International Ryukyu Karate Research Society.

Ravignat, M. (2004). The history of Goju-ryu karate: New ideas on Goju-ryu's direct Chinese ancestors. www.meibukanmagazine.org

chapter 7

Evaluating Makiwara Punching Board Performance

by Paul K. Smith, Ph.D., Timothy Niiler, Ph.D.,
& Peter W. McCullough, B.S.

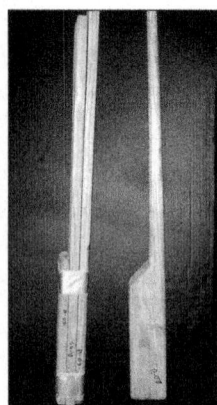

Dr. Paul Smith punching the makiwara board. **Figure 1:** Photos of stacked and tapered makiwara boards. The stacked makiwara design is comprised of several boards that are secured together, whereas the tapered makiwara design is comprised of a single molded piece of wood. *Illustrations courtesy of P. Smith except where noted.*

Introduction

Karate is a Japanese martial art offering the benefits of self-defense training for the practitioner, in addition to health-related, psychomotor, cognitive, and affective domain areas of development. As such, it is an excellent medium for physical education, plus the added value of learning practical skills. In karate training, punching and kicking are the two most often used techniques utilized to overcome an opponent. Characteristic of karate punching and kicking is the principle of "one blow, one kill" (*ikken hitsatsu*), a Japanese concept which means that the practitioner should be capable of disabling an attacker with one blow (Okazaki and Stricevic, 1984)—not necessarily to "kill" the opponent. Of the estimated 50 million persons involved with karate training (Smith, 1984), it is probable that every participant will, at some point, be exposed to the phenomena of punching some type of device to enhance his/her skill and "get a feel" for what it is like to impact an object. *Makiwara* ("coiled straw," punching board) training is considered by many proponents of this traditional martial art to be an integral part of the development of proper karate punching technique to the necessary standards (Okazaki and Stricevic, 1984).

The makiwara board is a vertically mounted device, attached or buried at one end (Figure 1), which is used to develop punching effectiveness through repeatedly punching or striking a pad attached to the free end of the board. The pad is generally of some variety of foam, rope, straw, or textile material used to soften the impact on the knuckles. The board's shape may be tapered or stacked, and its dimensions are generally about 8.89 cm (3.5 in.) width by 127.00 cm (50.00 in.) height above the floor. General physical principles imply that the type of wood used, its length, and the board's degree of taper should determine the strength of the "spring" of the device. Another popular design consists of various lengths of boards stacked in descending order of length to create a leaf-spring configuration. Several species of hardwoods or softwoods have been used. Usually, the student selects the boards to train with on the basis of personal preference or what boards are available in the training hall (Okazaki, 1998).

The mechanism by which the board helps develop punching proficiency involves the coordination of the body's movements such that the "force" or "energy" is concentrated, or focused, at a particular point within the impacted target. This is usually about 5.08-15.24 cm (2 to 6 inches) deep to the target surface and requires timing the puncher's segmental motions to impact the target with his weapon mass, body inertia connected to the fist or foot, moving at an optimum velocity at the time of impact. Impacts of varying characteristics are required to stop an assailant dependent on which part of the body is involved. Impacts can be characterized both in terms of mass-velocity relationships, such as "high velocity/low mass" or "low velocity/high mass," and the nature of the movement of the impacting weapon in applying force, e.g., linear or angular application of force. Punching is considered a relatively low velocity/high mass technique in which the force is applied in a linear fashion (Smith, et al., 1993). The fist and forearm are thrust in a "push-like" manner into the target, rather than whipped or snapped into the target in a "throw-like" action (Kreighbaum and Barthels, 1996). This type of technique is better used for impacting the opponent's trunk, where a deeper penetration into relatively soft tissue or vulnerable bone is needed to break, accelerate, or lacerate the bones, nerves and tissues of the body. The throw-like action, commonly known as a strike or snapping technique, is used to attack harder or more fragile areas of the body, such as the nose or joints, and "shock" the impacted tissues beneath the surface or break the relatively fragile bone or joint harder tissues.

According to Smith (1999), the appropriate technique for punching or striking the makiwara would be to stand directly in front of the board in a stance of your choice and applying the force of the technique by "punching through" the pad on the board and holding the full penetration momentarily to allow the body to train the muscles and "focus," or concentrate the body's energy, at the end of the movement. Punching force should be mildly applied in the beginning and progress to harder punches as experienced is gained. The body would be adapting to the reaction forces, or load, of the board. Care should be used in driving through the surface of the target toward full extension of the technique and not "slapping" the board. This would allow the body to coordinate and develop the neuromuscular system for more effective execution of the techniques.

No specific training sequences, or periodization of training, have been published (Smith, 1999) for the number of sets and number of repetitions in each set for makiwara training. Based on the training principles of progression (McArdle, Katch, and Katch, 2001) and practical experience of the authors, it would seem reasonable to begin with a low number of sets and repetitions when impacting the makiwara board and progress to higher numbers of repetitions and loads. Similar progressive resistance training has been shown to be effective in improving kicking performance in taekwondo athletes (Jakubiak and Saunders, 2008).

Methods

A first step in determining the efficacy of makiwara boards for resistance training is to evaluate the stiffness characteristics of the board itself without human intervention. This may be done via the load-deflection technique in which the makiwara board is loaded with a series of known weights while measuring the resultant deflection. The load may be plotted versus the deflection to visualize stiffness which is defined as the slope of this curve. As a result, materials with steeper load-deflection curves are stiffer and resist deformation more easily. Understanding this, it is tempting to go and look up the stiffness of a given wood and draw conclusions as to which wood might be more appropriate to one's training level. An expert makiwara user might choose a stiffer wood than a beginner. However, this overlooks some key issues. First, the stiffness by itself says nothing about the amount of force it takes to deflect a board of a given shape or construction. An expert will have just as much trouble punching a fixed 4"x4" wooden beam as the layman regardless of wood type since this geometry has little flexibility. Thus, real testing of the shapes in question are needed to establish force benchmarks by wood and design. Second, it is necessary to test multiple instances of a type of wood and design to ensure reliability of results. Wood is quite variable by its nature, and its age, grain, and other factors can cause differences in stiffness.

Therefore, five replications each of northern white ash, Pennsylvania cherry, red oak, and Douglas fir makiwara boards of the tapered and stacked board designs were constructed for testing in a base/loading mechanism specifically designed for this purpose (Figure 2). Boards were tested by loading each with weights and recording deflection values at 111.2 N (25 lbs) increments of weight ranging from 111.2 N to 1000.8 N (25-225 lbs) in counterbalanced order to distribute any cumulative stress effects throughout the study. Force-deflection data were plotted for each board specie and design. Furthermore, lines of best fit that showed the average trends in stiffness for each board type were plotted to ease visual comparison between both specie and design.

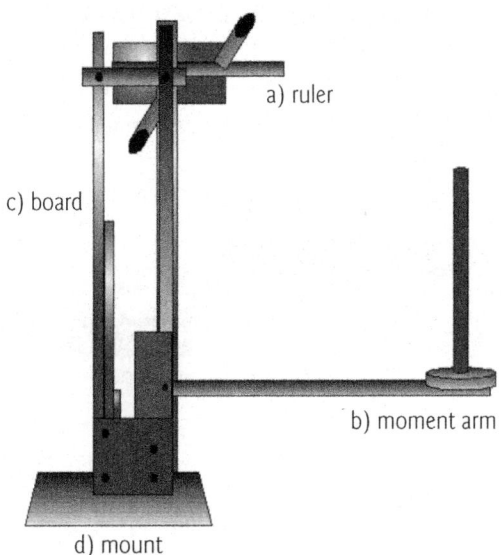

Figure 2: The makiwara device. A ruler (a) was clipped perpendicular to the makiwara board (c) to determine deflection. The loading device consisted of a moment arm (b) where weights could be placed to deflect the board. The mount (d) was set in concrete using lag bolts to ensure immobility of the base.

This method of viewing results has one drawback from a scientific perspective: despite visual trends one cannot tell whether differences in the slopes are the curves are significant or not. When we say that there is a significant difference between two groups, we are indicating that any differences observed between the groups is not a result of random chance alone. Without statistical significance, we often say that the result is anecdotal and we have no confidence that the results are repeatable. The statistical tool that is used in cases like this is the analysis of variance (ANOVA) which will determine if any significant differences exist among the designs or the species of wood. Given that such a difference exists, a post-hoc test identifies specifically which groups are different from one another.

Results

General results are summarized in Tables 1, 2, and 3. Table 1 presents results in the form of combined makiwara board deflection means (mm) of ash, cherry, fir, and oak species for stacked (ST) and tapered (TA) board types (BDTYP). Deflection means (mm) for stacked makiwara boards are shown by specie in Table 2 while those for tapered boards are shown in Table 3. Specie of wood is abbreviated as ash (A), cherry (C), fir (F) and oak (O). The differences in numbers of boards of each specie are due to breakage. Our use of a 2x4 ANOVA (two types of boards by four types of wood) with a Neuman-Keuls post-hoc tests indicated that there was, in fact, a significant difference between force-deflection properties of all groups except for the tapered ash and cherry boards.

TABLE 1

Wood	N	Mean	Std Dev
ST	156	102	68*
TA	180	65	46

$* p < 0.05$

TABLE 2

Wood	N	Mean	Std Dev
C	41	118	74*
A	36	106	71*
F	34	94	64*
O	45	90	59

$* p < 0.05$

TABLE 3

Wood	N	Mean	Std Dev
C	45	78	54*
A	45	76	52*
F	45	55	36*
O	45	50	33

$* p < 0.05$

TABLE 4

Wood	Board Tapered (N/m)	Type Stacked (N/m)
C	5389 ± 10	3907 ± 19
A	5253 ± 9	3245 ± 6
F	8096 ± 4	3985 ± 11
O	8653 ± 7	4882 ± 13

Discussion of Trends

Further examination of results indicated a number of noteworthy trends. Tapered boards showed significantly less flexure upon loading than did stacked boards (Table 1). This is not surprising since there is no horizontal binding force other than friction in between the stacked boards. This allows the stacked boards to slide with respect to one another under loading unlike the tapered boards that do not have this degree of freedom. As such, there is a greater mobility of the striking surface in the stacked board design. A consequence of this mobility is that the stacked boards will more readily approach their elastic limit in deflection after which they will either not return to their original shape or experience fracture. In actual fact, breakage occurred quite frequently in the more compliant stacked boards. Specifically, four of the stacked fir boards broke (80%), all five of the stacked ash boards broke (100%), and two of the stacked cherry boards broke (40%). None of the oak boards broke and none of the boards broke at the lowest load (111.2 N).

Dr. Paul Smith punching the makiwara board.

Stacked Board

Figure 3: Force-deflection curves for stacked boards. Boards that deflect less under a given load are considered to be stiffer. Significant differences in average force and average deflection were detected between each type of stacked board.

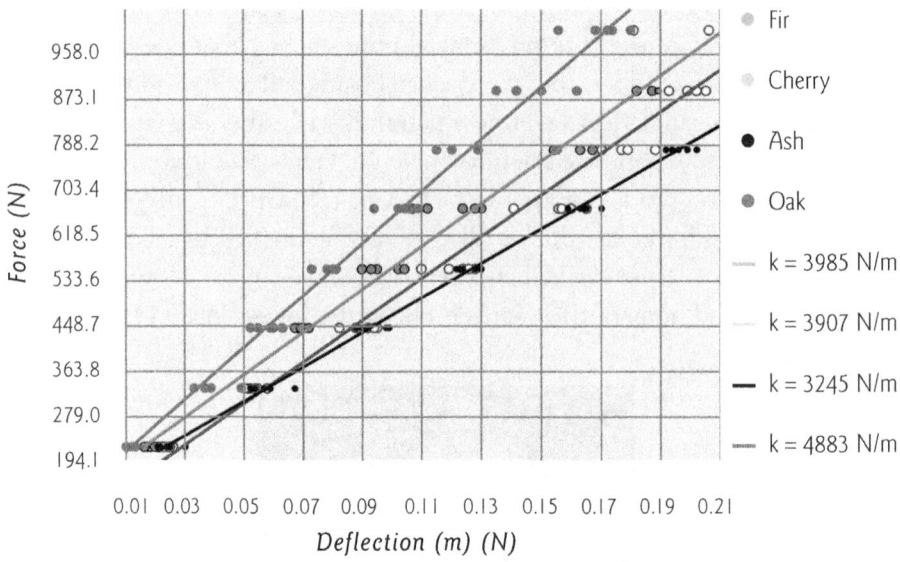

When boards were analyzed according to specie, for both tapered and stacked board types, oak had the least average deflection followed by fir, cherry, and ash (Tables 2-3). This is inconsistent with average impact bending parameters from the material data sheets in that one would expect ash to be stiffer and fir to be more compliant (Green, et al., 1999). However, since the impact bending parameter may vary as much as 25% for a given board type, the results are realistic. Furthermore, the similarity of results from board to board of the same specie is due to these boards having been made from the same tree. Stiffness calculated from the best fit load/deflection lines (Figures 3-4) show the same trends as with average deflections with oak being the stiffest wood and ash being the most compliant (Table 4).

Implications for Training

When viewed in light of the well-known recommendations of progressive overload in sports training (McArdle, Katch, and Katch 2001), this study's results are suggestive of a facility for the progression of training for appropriate development. The lower stiffness (by a factor of two) of stacked boards implies

Tepered Board

Figure 4: Force-deflection curve for tapered boards. Significant differences were detected between each type of tapered board except between Ash and Cherry ($p < 0.05$).

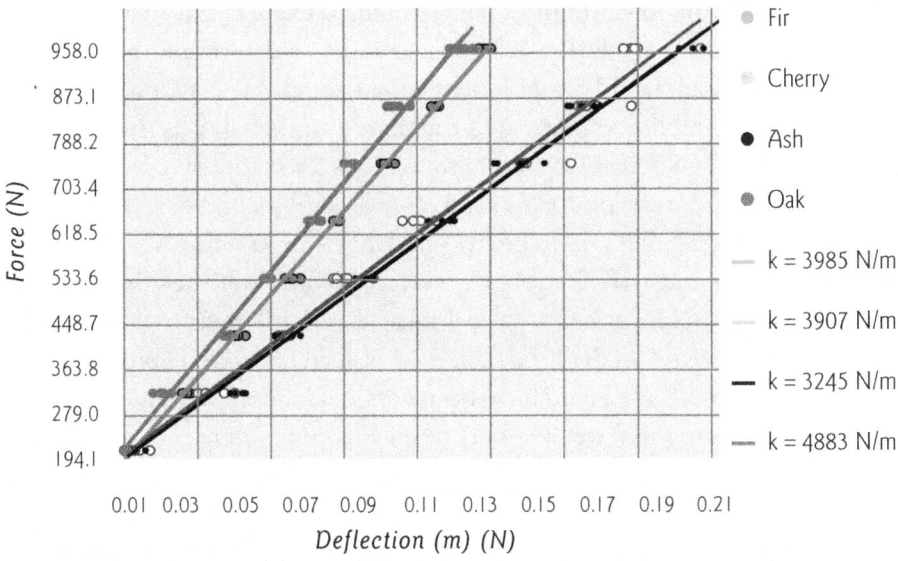

a greater suitability for novice practitioner as these will offer less resistance and lower reaction forces to the punch. For truly progressive training, one could start with the most compliant wood type (ash) and move up toward the stiffest (oak). However, in consideration of the breakage of all wood types of stacked boards except oak, perhaps only oak should be considered as a material for this design. Although oak has a higher stiffness, this could be modulated by varying the thickness of the boards or the addition of extra padding at the striking surface. More advanced practitioners could then move to the tapered design for increased resistance training.

This study also provides, by means of the quantification of makiwara board force-deflection curves, a standards-based way to estimate the workload associated with a given practice regimen. The American College of Sports Medicine (ACSM) regularly publishes a paper titled "Progression Models in Resistance Training" that is a summary of current best practice in designing strength training workouts. According to this document's the most recent update (ACSM, 2009), resistance training for beginners should be 60-70% of the one repetition maximum (1RM) of a given exercise. A standard exercise that is similar to the reverse punch is the bench press. If one could press 225 lbs for ones 1RM (using two arms), half of this is 112.5 lbs. Seventy percent of the one arm maximum load is 78.75 lbs or 351 N. So, if one were using the more compliant stacked cherry makiwara, the deflection corresponding to this load would be about 6 cm or about 2.3 inches. Considering that the punch is actually dynamic, a greater deflection would probably occur; but this estimation sets the lower limit of what would be expected of such a person. Alternatively, this calculation could be reversed to determine the most appropriate makiwara board for an individual based on their 1RM bench press.

Having established a way to estimate the workload, it is then possible to apply ACSM guidelines regarding repetitions for progressive training. Although many different protocols exist, the generally cited 8-12 repetitions with multiple sets still seems to be the standard for beginners (ACSM, 2009). Recent meta-analysis of 37 strength training studies indicates that gains in strength are optimized at eight sets per muscle group (Peterson, et al., 2005). However, because no studies of the efficacy of such an exercise protocol with respect to the makiwara board have been conducted, it may be that increased repetitions per set and fewer sets may be equally productive.

Conclusions

It can be concluded from our findings that there were differences between the makiwara designs and differences among the wood types tested. The tapered board design was stiffer than the stacked configuration; however there was no difference between the cherry and ash makiwara with the tapered design. Makiwara stiffness was progressively less from oak to fir to ash to cherry wood boards. A logical progression for training would be to begin with the stacked design of one of the lesser stiff woods to makiwara made in the tapered design of one of the stiffer woods. Based on the force-deflection curves, it is also possible to roughly estimate workload and thereby design an effective resistance training program.

一拳必殺	*ikken hitsatsu*	"one blow, one kill"
巻藁	*makiwara*	"coiled straw"

References

American College of Sports Medicine (2009 March). American College of Sports Medicine position stand. Progression models in resistance training for healthy adults. *Medicine and Science in Sports and Exercise*, 41(3): 687-708.

Green, D., Winandy, J., and Kretschmann, D. (1999). *Wood handbook: Wood as an engineering material*. Madison, WI: USDA Forest Service, Forest Products Laboratory. General technical report FPL; GTR-113: Pages 4.1-4.45.

Kreighbaum, E., and Barthels, K. (1996). *Biomechanics: A qualitative approach for studying human movement* (4th Ed.). Needham Heights, MA: Allyn and Bacon.

McArdle, W., Katch F., and Katch V. (2001). *Exercise physiology: Energy, nutrition and human performance*. Baltimore, MA: Lippincott, Williams & Wilkins.

Okazaki, T. (1998). Personal communication. ISKF Headquarters Dojo, 222 S. 45th St., Philadelphia, PA, 19104.

Okazaki, T., and Stricevic, M. (1984). *Textbook of modern karate*. Tokyo: Kodansha International.

Peterson, M., Rhea, M., and Alvar, B. (2005). Applications of the dose response for muscular strength development: A review of metaanalytic efficacy and reliability for designing training prescription. *Journal of Strength and Conditioning Research*, 19: 950-8.

Stricevic, M., Dacic, D., Miyazaki, T., and Anderson, G. (1989). *Modern karate: A scientific approach to conditioning and training*. Rockville Centre, NY: Miroto Karate Publishing Co.

Smith, P., Viano, D., Faust, D., and Faust, L. (1993). Thoracic injury effects of linear and angular karate impact. In *Biomechanics in Sports XI.*, Hamill, J., Derrick, T., and Elliott, E. (Eds.), Amherst, MA: International Society of Biomechanics in Sports.

Smith, P. (1984). Selected impact characteristics of karate and boxing gloves. Unpublished doctoral dissertation. Southern Illinois University at Carbondale, Carbondale, IL.

chapter 8

Attention, Sit, Meditate, Bow, Ready Position: Ritualized Dojo Pattern or Character Training?

by Marvin Labbate

Photography courtesy of M. Labbate.

The Ritualized Pattern at the Start of Class

The *dojo*, literally translated, means "Way place." It is the place to learn the Way. An explanation of the Way is a topic deserving of its own paper, but for our dojo it is the development of mind, body, and spirit through the study of traditional Okinawan Goju-ryu karatedo. The dojo reflects the philosophy of our past and present masters who are peaceful, loving, spiritual people. The environment of the dojo is extremely influential on the spiritual and focused mind-set of the students. We do not want to walk into a chaotic environment that is distracting and adds to the anxiety of our day. The dojo should be serene, stark, and clean. The dojo is our sanctuary for learning and developing our total being.

The white uniform, which was adopted from judo, founded by Kano Jigoro (1860-1938), is a symbol of purity, perfection, and equality. Students and instructors should dress in clean, crisp uniforms. Changing into a clean uniform is a physical, outward expression of the mental, spiritual, and physical development we are striving for through our karate training. We are shedding our "old" clothes and cleansing ourselves of anxieties and events that can distract us during training. Putting on a clean uniform is rejuvenating and helps prepare us for training.

The preclass period at the dojo is a time for talking to fellow students, stretching, and mentally unwinding. There is a Chinese proverb that says, "Empty your cup before you fill it." We can't come to class with a full cup. We must leave our egos outside the dojo and put our day behind us if we are to approach our training and each other with humility, openness, and willingness to learn. It is very difficult to teach and to learn if we have inflated egos, are closed minded, or are distracted by life outside of the dojo.

At the start of class, students are instructed to *shugo*, which translates as "to gather around" but is used to mean "line up." Shugo, as well as the other elements of the ritualized pattern, can be broken down into physical and mental components. Physically, the students are simply lining up in rows. It is the transition from the free-flowing preclass time to the structured class time. After the students have properly lined up, they immediately stand in a ready position (*yoi*). The students are standing with their feet firmly planted in a parallel stance (*heiko dachi*), their eyes looking forward, and hands clenched by their sides (figure 1). Lining up in a ready position sends the mental signal to the students that class is beginning and it is time to prepare. When the students are lining up, they are mentally aware of and adhering to the tradition of lining up by rank, designated by belt color. The ranking system, also developed by Kano Jigoro, was adopted with the systemization of karate. The higher-ranking students line up in the front of the class, followed by intermediate and beginner students. A student's position in the line places responsibilities on him or her. For example, a student in the middle of the group must show the proper respect and etiquette to the senior students, be responsible for his own training, and be an example to the junior students who are watching. Maintaining neat, orderly lines throughout class enhances the nonchaotic, concise atmosphere of the dojo. The instructor then tells the students to come to attention (*kiotsuke*) (figure 2). Kiotsuke, when broken down, literally means, "Take your *ki*, or energy, and bring your full attention to the training and the present moment" (Opdam, 2007). Physically, the students are in a stance with heels together (*masubi dachi*), toes pointing out at a 45-degree angle, and their hands are open by their sides. The back is straight, the chin is pulled in, and the eyes are focused straight ahead toward the *shomen* wall (the wall of honor within a dojo). This phase of class is extremely important because the physical posture just described is conducive to listening, focusing, and committing students' full attention to the instructor. The students are engaged at a heightened level of awareness, bringing mind and body to attention.

Still at attention (*kiotsuke*), the students and instructor do a standing bow (*rei*), bending from the waist and keeping their backs straight. This bow is a common courtesy to show respect to our fellow companions. It is a general greeting and a show of good manners likened to the western custom of shaking hands and saying hello. After bowing, everyone returns to attention. The students are then instructed to sit (*seiza*), which was once the respectful, formal way of sitting adopted by the warrior class in Japan. The instructor and students lower themselves to their left knee, then their right, to a kneeling position seated back on their heels (figure 3). Their backs are straight, chins pulled in; their tongues are on the hard upper palate, and their hands are resting on their legs. The instructor will then say, "*mokuso*" (meditate), which can be thought of as the mental component of seiza sitting. When the instructor says mokuso, the students close their eyes and begin to meditate or "clear one's mind," breathing in deeply through the nose, drawing in energy, and moving this energy to their physical center (*tanden*) (figure 4). Alternatively, students may choose to reflect on their training by asking themselves some of the following questions. What corrections did I receive last class? Have I tried to incorporate these corrections into my training? Have I improved? Do I need to focus on the same corrections again? Students may choose to use this time to reflect on their spiritual development or to pray. Yagi Meitoku (1912-2003; 10th-degree ranking in Goju-ryu Meibukan) had many dojo rules that he taught his students as part of their spiritual training. One of the many is "*Oku myo zai ren shin*," which means, "The secret techniques come from having a good heart," or "Train your spirit to be a good person" (Yagi, et al., 1998). A student may want to reflect on his or her responsibilities as a karate practitioner. Does he set a good example to other students? Does he live by the dojo principles and treat family, neighbors, co-workers, and strangers with respect and humility? Just as putting on a clean white uniform is an act of outward cleansing, meditating (*mokuso*) is an act of inner cleansing. Students can also choose to reflect on or pray for any particular need they may have on that day.

For the class instructor, this can be a time to reflect on the class he or she is about to teach and how to best communicate with the students. When I am teaching class, I pray to God as my personal form of reflection. I pray for my students. I pray that I can teach them techniques in the most effective yet safe way so that no one is injured. In viewing myself as a servant, I pray that the students will benefit from training, be it physically, mentally, or spiritually. I use this time to reflect on my character. Am I a good role model? Do I demonstrate good moral character through my teaching? Am I teaching to be a blessing to my students, or am I teaching to satisfy my ego? Many of us may not have the self-discipline to spiritually "work out" on our own, so this can be the perfect time to reshape our inner being through meditation and reflection.

Several aspects of meditation (*mokuso*), when considered together, can be overwhelming to a student. One does not have to reflect on every aspect of his mental, physical, and spiritual development every class. What one reflects on specifically may change with the day. What is important, then, is to find and reflect on weaknesses you are feeling at a given moment and ask yourself what you need to do to improve and strengthen your inner self. A minimum of three to five minutes of meditation is crucial in preparing for training and should not be skimmed over. By the time the instructor says, "*Mokuso yame*" (stop meditating), each student should have a clear connection between mind and body. Students and the instructor are now fully engaged in a learning mind-set, ready to continue with their physical training.

The final element of the ritualized pattern goes back to the bow (*rei*), but with different physical and mental components. Bowing is done from sitting in the seiza posture. Facing the shomen wall, the instructor says, "*Shomen ni rei*," which means, "Bow to the wall of honor." The instructor and students bow by bringing their left then right hands together on the floor directly in front of them (figure 5), then lowering their heads to their hands (figure 6).

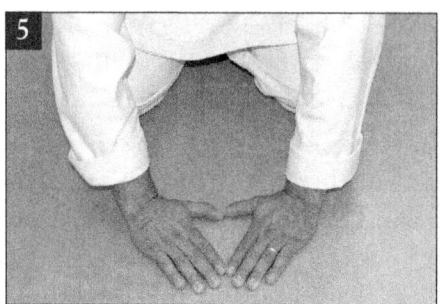

The simple physical act of bowing encompasses a wealth of meaning. Bowing to the shomen wall is a sign of respect, not worship, for past and current masters. Mentally, we are acknowledging the traditions, wisdom, and insight the masters have passed on to us. Traditional karate can be likened to our parents, grandparents, and great grandparents who have shared traditions, family history, and wisdom with successive generations. This natural family model is the basis for the karate family that has developed over many, many years. The early karate masters believed in the family unit and considered their karate students as family and as the means for passing on coveted knowledge to future generations. Traditional Okinawan karate has survived the centuries because our past masters believed in its value and were committed to sharing karate in its entirety.

There is a spiritual aspect of bowing to the shomen wall as well. Each dojo has a unique shomen wall, usually containing some element of spirituality. At my dojo, there is a cross representing Christianity on the shomen wall. If I have been praying, I am humbling myself and bowing to the Lord when I bow to the shomen wall. Bowing to the shomen wall is a private exercise, and the intent of the individual's bow depends on his or her faith, beliefs, and mind-set. Bowing is also a sign of respect for the dojo. It is an outward expression of an inward responsibility. Students and instructors alike are responsible for maintaining an environment conducive to learning by reflecting on their surroundings. Does the dojo reflect the traditions and philosophy of Okinawan karate? Is the dojo clean, tidy, stark, and serene? Paying attention to such details trains us to be visually aware of our surroundings, which will carry over to our everyday life. Adherence to the rules of the dojo is an effective yet subtle way to cultivate responsibility and self-discipline both inside and outside of the dojo.

After the instructor and students have bowed to the shomen wall, the instructor turns to face the students, and the highest-ranking students say, "*Rei*" (bow). The instructor and students bow to each other, saying, "*Onegai shimasu*," meaning, "Please teach me" (figure 7). Learning is a mutual process for the instructor and the students. The instructor enters training humble, empty, willing to learn through teaching, and showing the utmost respect to his or her students. The students bow to the instructor as a sign of respect. As we get to know our instructors, we gain a sincere respect for their knowledge, insight of the art, and their overall character. In this regard, when the students bow to the instructor and he to them, it is at a deeper, more personal level. Everyone now stands up and goes back to the ready position (*yoi*). The students are now physically, mentally, and spiritually prepared to train.

Students are frequently brought back to the ready position between drills and exercises. This is a time to reconnect the body and mind through focus and deep breathing. When students get tired, they are often easily distracted, making it important to draw them back to a learning mind-set and to refocus on the lesson.

The Ritualized Pattern as it Applies to Solo Training

The next segment of class is the lesson the instructor has planned, which may focus on solo training, partner training, or both. Before the lesson begins, the instructor and students will perform a ritualized pattern that differs somewhat from the one done at the beginning of class. It is, however, made up of the same elements: ready posture, attention, bow, meditate, and back to the ready posture. It is essential that this routine be incorporated into your karate training, whether you are practicing alone or as an individual in a group. Performing this routine at the start and conclusion of kata, drills, or partner drills helps establish the mind-set of learning. Training at the dojo is done in the context of learning, often through self-discovery, and developing mentally, physically, and spiritually.

A *kata* is a formalized sequence of martial self-defense moves performed like a dance or shadow boxing, often done solo. At the start of kata training, the students are in a ready position while respectfully waiting for instructions (figure 8). When the instructor announces *kiotsuke* (attention), the students physically move to an attention stance, as previously described (figure 9). Mentally, each student is focused, actively listening and visually aware. Next the instructor and class do a standing bow, again saying, "*Onegai shimasu*" (Please teach me) (figure 10). Similar to the bow at the beginning of class, the students perform this bow as an act of respect for the instructor, but it also holds a deeper meaning. The instructor and the students alike are acknowledging a level of seriousness for their karate training. The students engage their minds and bodies in a serious, introspective approach to analyze principles, movement, and self-defense applications. Before performing the kata, the students center their energy (*mokuso*), in a standing position. The students bring both hands up to approximately chest level, with fingers pointing up, and breathe in deeply through the nose, gathering their energy (figure 11). The palm of the left hand is placed on the back of the right hand so that the knuckle of the right middle finger presses against the *laogong* pressure point (PC8), located between the second and third metacarpal bones of the left palm (figure 12) (Montaigue and Simpson, 1998). While exhaling and with the hands maintaining contact, the hands are rotated so that the fingers point downward. At the same time, the hands are moved down to the center of the body (*tanden* 丹田) (figure 13). The rotation of the knuckle against the *laogong* point of the palm activates an energy channel. Air, breath, and mind move to the center, and from this point forward, our mind and movement remain at our center. The final component of the ritualized pattern for solo training is what I refer to as a heightened ready position (*yoi*)—an "I'm ready" position of confidence.

While the foundation of training rests in respect and courtesy, the practice of harmonizing mind, body, and breath is also critical to training. Learning to harmonize each element follows the same process as learning a

kata. As novices, we learn gross motor movements and concentrate on memorizing the routine. As we advance in our training, we start thinking about the Sanchin kata principles of structure and movement and begin to incorporate them into our kata training (Labbate, 1999). Likewise, the ritualized pattern advances to a higher level in which static meditation transitions to moving meditation. Breathing and centering remain the same, but we now harmonize our breathing with movement.

Upon completion of the kata, the students meditate again to gather and center their energy, calm down, and reestablish the mind-body connection through deep breathing. They bring their hands to their sides, do a standing bow, and say, "*Domo arigato gozaimasu*," which means "Thank you," and is an outward expression of gratitude for the lessons learned and what they have discovered about their kata. A student's level of mental endurance will dictate the number of repetitions of a kata that can be done during a training session. Performing a kata or any drill at one hundred percent effort is mentally tiring, but mental endurance will develop with consistent training, just as with physical endurance.

The Ritualized Pattern and Partner Training

The physical, mental, and spiritual aspects of solo training also apply to partner training with an added layer of complexity as a result of working with another person. Training with a partner is advanced and takes on new principles on all three levels. Partners line up facing each other in the ready position and perform the same ritualized pattern of coming to attention, bowing, meditating, and returning to a ready position before starting the drill (figure 14). This is the point when partners make eye contact with each other. Eye contact is critical in partner training because it is the initial way to create and fully engage in a connection between partners. After coming to attention, each partner is alert and focused on the other person (figure 15). This is a time to "size up" your partner. How do your height, weight, and reach compare? What kind of adjustments might you have to make to compensate for physical differences? What is your partner's skill level? These are all important observations to consider.

The next component of the ritualized pattern is the bow (figure 16). Unlike the other bows, the bow in partner training is unique and specific. Partners bow to each other to demonstrate mutual respect, modesty, humility, and harmony. When the students say, "*Onegai shimasu*" to each other, they are saying, "Please trust that I will care for you." There is a maxim that accurately describes the essence of partner training: *jita kyoei*, 自他共栄—mutual welfare and benefit (Watanabe, et al., 1972). Partners are entering into a level of training with high regard for each other's progress and safety so that each will benefit. Partner training is never one sided, even between beginner and advanced students. The higher-skill-level student takes on a mentoring role and will learn through teaching, whereas the lower-skill-level student will learn from one-on-one time with his or her partner. Neither student is a punching bag or a target for the other's ego. After bowing, the students remain in the bow position. The instructor announces the drill and says, "*mokuso*" (meditate). The students perform mokuso as they would kata training, drawing in and centering their energy and concentrating on connecting with their partner (figures 17–18). The mind-body connection between partners is much more complicated than the mind-body connection an individual develops within him- or herself. There is a physical, mental, and spiritual awareness between partners that develops with repeated partner training.

We discussed the physical awareness partners have of each other and went into a bit more detail discussing the spiritual aspects of partner training; now let us explore mental awareness. This refers to a mutual understanding partners have of each other's emotional state and the effect partners have on each other. For example, failing to shed anxiety during meditation can be distracting to the person you are working with. It is important to give 100 percent of your attention and effort to your partner. Sense your partner's mental and emotional state. Is he or she approaching this training with the same level of seriousness, intensity, and humility as you? Is your partner nervous or anxious? Awareness and sensitivity to your partner's emotional and mental status is paramount in partner training. Ultimately, students will develop the sense of mental control needed for physical control.

Dialogue between partners during drills is a unique aspect of partner training that is mutually beneficial. If partners perceive there is a disconnect between them, they can stop, determine the reason, and then concentrate on reestablishing the connection. Partner training will expose each other's weaknesses. Through honest, humble dialogue, the students can help each other correct and understand techniques. This not only elevates each other's skill development but also aids in building a bond of trust between partners.

During partner training and upon completion of the formal partner drills, the students come back to the ready posture to re-establish the mind-body connection as individuals and as partners. When partner training ends, the students maintain eye contact, come to attention, and then bow, saying, "*Domo arigato gozaimasu.*" The students are offering a genuine "thank you" for the time spent with each other, the mutual benefits each received through this training, and for the positive impact the partners have on each other because of their humble, respectful attitude.

The Ritualized Pattern at the End of Class

At the end of class, the same ritualized pattern as that done at the beginning of class is performed. The students and instructor line up in a ready position, move to the seated position, and meditate. As with the beginning of class, the students can use this time for meditation, reflection, or prayer. When I am the class instructor, I pray that the students have benefited from the class and are leaving feeling better in some way, be it mentally or physically. Perhaps something a student had been struggling to understand or perform became clear and achievable. Students should reflect on the class they just participated in. Some questions they might ask themselves include the following: Did I remember the corrections from last class and try to improve? Did I receive any new corrections or new information to incorporate into my training? After meditation, the instructor and students bow to the shomen wall. Again, as at the beginning of class, they are honoring the past karate masters. Additionally, this bow serves as a reminder that as students and instructors we have the responsibility to pass down the knowledge that has been given to us. The price we pay for studying karate is to share this knowledge in its original form and meaning. It is through the giving/receiving relationships of instructors to students and students to students that this knowledge is passed on. The instructor then faces the students. They bow to each other, offering a mutual, genuine thank you by saying, "*Domo arigato gozaimasu.*" The students should be thanking the instructor for the time he or she has donated. The gift of time is priceless in and of itself and it is through this gift that the art of karate is passed on from generation to generation. Students may not know and appreciate this at first, but as they get to know the instructors, *domo arigato gozai-masu* will come to mean much more than thank you for the karate lesson. As the instructor, I am thanking the students for the knowledge I have gained through teaching and for allowing me to touch their hearts in some way. For as many people as I teach on any day, I have the responsibility to be pure of heart and to impact people in a positive way. Funakoshi Gichin (1868–1957) wrote in the first of the Twenty Precepts: "Karate-do begins with courtesy and ends with a bow." Ultimately, we will learn that it is this higher level of thankfulness and gratitude that keeps us humble. Being humble drives us to constantly strive to learn and improve.

• • •

We have explored the origin and meaning of each component of the ritualized pattern and why it is performed at the beginning of class, during solo and partner training, and at the end of class. We've also explained that there are physical, mental, and spiritual aspects to each component that develop and deepen in meaning with practice. The ritual in and of itself is training, which, with a full understanding and continuous practice, will further enhance the student's skill level. It is my hope that you now have a better understanding of the significance of the exercise that appears to be a simple ritual.

References

Labbate, M. (1999). Elements of advanced karate technique. *Journal of Asian Martial Arts*, 8(2): 80-95.

Montaigue, E., and Simpson, W. (1997). *The encyclopedia of dim-mak*. Boulder, CO: Paladin Press.

Opdam, L. (2007). *Karate Goju Ryu Meibukan*. Los Angeles, CA: Empire Books.

Watanabe, J., and Avakian, L. (1972). *The secrets of judo: A text for instructors and students*. Rutland, VT: Charles E. Tuttle Co.

Yagi, M., Wheeler, C., and Vickerson, B. (1998). *Okinawan Karate-Do Gojyu-Ryu Meibu-Kan*. Charlottetown, PE, Canada: Action Press.

chapter 9

Issues Concerning Board Breaking

by Phil Davison, M.A.

The author breaking an unsupported board.
Photographs courtesy of P. Davison.

Once when Kyuzo Mifune visited a karate dojo, he was shown a demonstration of tile-breaking by one of the karate men. After the karate man had smashed a number of tiles piled on top of each other, he asked Mifune, "Can a Judo man do this?"

"Yes, it is very easy," Mifune replied.

"Is that so? Can we see what kind of technique a Judo man uses?" the karate man challenged.

"Of course. Please set up the tiles. I'll be back in a minute," Mifune instructed. Mifune returned with a hammer he had brought along in his bag.

"You are not going to use that to break the tiles, are you?" the karate man protested.

"Yes. I told you it was easy. Efficient use of energy is a key principle of Judo."
—John Stevens, 2001: 107

Arthritis

It has become clear that osteoarthritis is not an inevitable disease of aging: osteoarthritis is associated with some occupations more than others. For example, a 2003 Quebec study demonstrated clear links between occupations involving manual labour and the onset of osteoarthritis (Rossignol, 2004). What we do to our limbs may return to haunt us in later life. The aforementioned study showed the peak prevalence of symptoms in men was in the 70-to-79-year age bracket.

There are few longitudinal studies focusing on the relation of injury to development of osteoarthritis. One study, the Johns Hopkins Precursors Study, followed a large cohort from young adulthood into old age, and was able to demonstrate a relationship between injury and the onset of arthritis (Gelber, 2000). In this study 1,321 medical students were tracked over several decades, and it was shown that an injury to the knee in youth or middle age resulted in nearly three times (the actual figure is 2.95) the likelihood of developing osteoarthritis in later life.

However, the Johns Hopkins study focused on easily measureable injuries, such as dislocation or fracture. The sort of injury sustained in breaking boards is less severe, but more repeated. One does not break a leg regularly, yet some people will perform *tamashiwari* (testing one's combat skills by breaking objects) as often as monthly. The effects of repeated low-level trauma are more difficult to assess outside of a martial arts environment—ethics committee approval to get a cohort to regularly smash their limbs into hard objects is not easily forthcoming—and outside of a martial arts environment it is hard to conceive of people who could be persuaded to act in such a way.

To further complicate matters, there are a surprising variety of results concerning exercise and the risk of osteoarthritis, showing both increased and decreased risk. Heesch et al. found that light exercise tended to lessen the risk of arthritis in older women but not in middle aged women (Heesch, 2007).[1] Other studies, such as that by Carol Teitz, have shown an increased risk of developing osteoarthritis in elite athletes and dancers (Teitz, 1998). Chakravarty (2008) found little difference in the risk of developing arthritis between long-distance runners and a control group over a period of twenty years.

Differences among individuals should also be taken into account, especially in regard to the difficulty of board breaks. Women have significantly lower bone mass and density. Van der Sluis (2002) measured the total bone mineral content of women at the age of twenty-two to have a mean of 2,790 g, compared with 3,515 g for men of the same age. Moreover, the difference between the largest male total bone mineral content is much more than twice that of the smallest female: around 4,700 g for the largest male compared with around 1,800 for the smallest female.

The Physics of Striking

Angelo Armenti has analyzed the force needed to break bone and concluded that there is significantly less force involved in breaking bone than in one of the standard boards used today (Armenti, 1992). In Ameneti's analysis it takes 3,111 N to break a pine board 300 mm x 200 mm x 10 mm. A board like this would be much easier to break than the standard boards in common use (300 mm x 300 mm x 20 mm—probably around twice as hard to break, if not harder). In Armenti's analysis he claims that breaking a bone with a 10 mm radius, 200 mm long, supported at both ends, should take 3,142 N.

Unfortunately, Armenti's analysis is seriously flawed. John Currey describes the difficulty in measuring Young's modulus of rupture for bone in a laboratory setting (Currey, 2002). This is compounded by the fact that the bone *in vivo* is surrounded by muscle, usually in motion, and definitely not supported at both ends. Bone is composed of different materials (compact and cancellous), which respond to forces differently and, in particular, cancellous bone responds to force differently at the ends compared to the middle of the bone. "The assumption [of fracture mechanics] is that any part of the material will behave linearly elastic until it ruptures. This is certainly not true for bone."

Since it is not possible to define accurately the amount of force required to break living bone, it is not possible to state that the force required to break a board is greater (or less) than that required to break a bone, but rather that the force required to break bone is highly unpredictable. This is borne out by anecdotal evidence from sparring accidents in the dojo: a blow with tremendous force can land on someone, knock him over, and yet cause no injury, yet a light blow at the correct angle on a vulnerable target is capable of causing serious injury.

To analyze an effective strike, from a power point of view, it is an oversimplification to use the kinetic energy equation ($1/2\ mv^2$). We must look at the momentum of the striking arm, the mass of the limb, the degree of connectedness the limb has to the rest of the body, the momentum of the body, and the degree of connectedness the body has with the ground, the hardness of the limb, and finally the momentum of the target. If we label the degree of connectedness as "transference," we can say that the key factors are mass, transference, velocity, hardness, and the momentum of the target.

Mass is not a straightforward item to measure in regard to punching.

The weight of the limb striking is not really relevant to measure—measuring just the limb would only be appropriate if measuring a severed limb thrown at the target. A skilled striker is able to transfer energy from the body to the striking limb, effectively putting more mass into the strike (i.e., he has greater skill at transference). A skilled striker is able to generate considerably more transference than an unskilled person. In everyday language we could say someone is putting his or her whole body into the strike.

A second form of transference is the ability of the striker to brace himself against the ground when striking. Since, in Newtonian physics, every action has an equal and opposite reaction, it is essential that the striker be grounded to propel him- or herself into the punch. For example, someone standing on a slippery surface will have a great deal of difficulty in propelling himself into a strike.

Velocity is an important variable in that the equation for kinetic energy reveals it to be squared—a small increase in velocity results in a big increase in power. Certainly there is a difference of velocity between skilled and unskilled strikers, yet the difference between the slowest and fastest punch of people with at least a little training is probably not enough to make a large difference in the force applied to the board.

For example, a typical skilled person can punch at around 9 meters per second. Assuming that an unskilled person's punch travels as slow as 7 meters per second[2] and, although perhaps unrealistically, that a person could put 100% of his body weight behind a punch[3], we can calculate the energy produced by slow and fast punches from people of different body weights.

Mass (halved)	Velocity (squared)	Resulting Energy
90 kg	9 mps	3645 j
90 kg	7 mps	2205 j
50 kg	9 mps	2025 j
50 kg	7 mps	1225 j

As can be seen in the table above, the difference between a fast and slow punch is less than the difference created by people of different body weights. If we compare the differences between 9 mps punches and 7 mps punches the results are 1,400 j at 90 kg (3,645 j less 2,205 j) and 800 j at 50 kg (2,025 j less 1,225 j). By contrast, the difference between the resulting energy figures between different body weights is 1,620 j at 9 mps (3,645 less 2,025 j), and 980 j at 7 mps (2205 j less 1,225 j).

The hardness of the objects being struck together determines which will be damaged by the impact. A one-kilogram sledgehammer striking a brick wall will damage the wall. A blob of jelly of the same weight, striking at the same velocity, will itself be damaged, leaving the wall undamaged. In punching terms this relates to the support of the muscular structures and to the density of the skeletal structures in the hand. Tensing the muscles on impact is one of the first skills learned from punching bags or focus mitts, but due to their lower bone density (Van der Sluis, 2002) women's bones are not as hard as men's and therefore are more at risk of injury when board breaking.

The momentum of the target is not really an issue in board breaking—the board is stationary and the mass is standardized. However, in self-defense situations the momentum of the target is a crucial factor in the impact delivered in a strike. A person who walks into a punch suffers a great deal more than someone who rolls with it.

We can see that, with training, a person can improve transference to get more mass behind the strike, and can increase punching velocity. Also with skill one can learn to adapt to situations where a punch is delivered when the opponent's momentum is optimal. This can enable a small person to "punch above her weight," i.e., to punch much harder than would be expected for a smaller person. However, purely in terms of power, the slightly built person is at a serious disadvantage when compared to a person with significantly more mass. A smaller person will never be able to match the power of a larger person who has similar skills.

This is not to say that smaller people cannot defend themselves. A smaller person may not be able to match the power of a larger person, but may have significant advantages in agility, and the many advantages of a better skill set gained through training far outweigh the advantage of being born with a larger body. Furthermore, breaking boards is an activity only tangentially connected to practical self-defense, in that boards do not move, do not fight back, and do not defend themselves—perhaps the primary skill in combat is the ability to overcome the opponent's defenses, and, in terms of striking, the primary skill is to delver the most appropriate strike for a given target, rather than the most powerful. The focus should not be on who is the most powerful, but rather on who can best deliver enough impact to the appropriate target to gain the desired effect.

It must also be said that a focus on power is misleading: the best punch is not the most powerful; it is the most appropriate. The ability to deliver a powerful punch is not useful if the punch elicits a defensive response from the enemy that means the punch does not land: a strike that is too powerful will not land, as it is more likely to provoke a defensive response. A light tap that does land on a vulnerable target can be effective in itself, and open the way (*suki*) by causing a momentary breach in the opponent's concentration, allowing more effective strikes.

Discussion

In the section on arthritis we can see that there is a link between injury and late-life arthritis. From the studies of risk of arthritis arising from different occupations we can see that repeated minor injury can also contribute to increased risk. Therefore, we can see that board breaking will cause some increase in risk, although it is not possible to say how much. We need to carefully weigh the unknown amount of risk of late-life arthritis with the benefits of breaking boards.

From the discussion of different body weights and bone densities we can see that board breaking is most certainly not a level playing field. A slightly built woman is likely to have a significantly harder time breaking boards than a strongly built man.

This raises the problem of a "standards based" approach to board breaking, if board breaking is included in a school's grading syllabus. Should we be saying that a person merits a certain grade because he can do a certain break (i.e., smaller people require a lot more skill than larger); or should we say that people of comparable skill level merit the grade (i.e., the breaking difficulty is adjusted to meet the body mass and/or gender of the student)?

The risk of a break failing is far greater for a slightly built person (regardless of gender) simply because of the lower mass striking the target. Should the break fail, the risk of injury, and of consequent late-life osteoarthritis, is far greater than if the break is successful. Women, with lower bone density are more at risk of injury than men, and doubly so because there is a greater element of risk of the break failing due to (on average) less lean body mass.

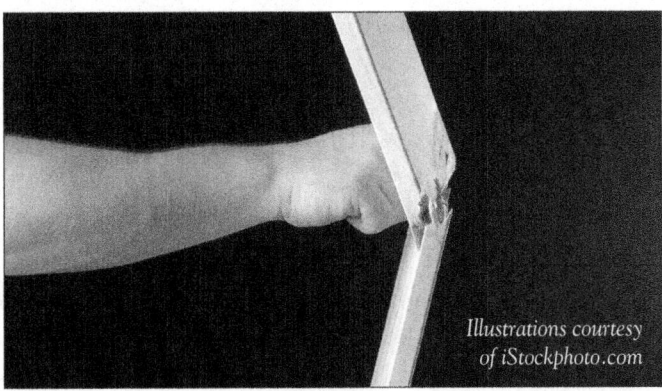

Illustrations courtesy of iStockphoto.com

Given the difference of skill levels required to perform the same break from people of widely different body weights and the increased risk of late-life arthritis, it would seem to me that any breaking syllabus should not be "one size fits all," and that the syllabus should change to meet individual needs.

There is a danger in emphasizing powerful strikes in that students come to regard power generation as more important than it really is for self-defense. Anyone should be able to knock an opponent down if that opponent stands still and does not defend him- or herself; a more significant skill is striking someone without raising his defenses. My concern is that excessive emphasis on power may hinder the ability to strike effectively (i.e., appropriately), and may actually reduce a student's fighting ability.

A partial solution could be the breaking of unsupported, lightly held boards. To break an unsupported board requires more skill, and especially more velocity, meaning there is less advantage in a higher body mass. Brute strength cannot break an unsupported board. Furthermore, the risk of injury is less, since a board that is not broken simply flies away with much less impact on the practitioner's hand. Repeated striking of unsupported boards, whether they break or not, may cause bruising, but is less likely to cause injury.

Appendix: Survey

In preparation for this essay I conducted an informal survey of people fifty years old or older who had been involved in board breaking in their youth. Unfortunately, there were only four respondents, meaning the sample size is too small to be anything other than anecdotal. Of the four respondents only one reported no issues with arthritis, two reported significant problems with arthritis that appeared to have no direct connection to board breaking, and the fourth reported issues with arthritis that could possibly have been related to board breaking. Given that in all cases the people had lived active lives, it is not really possible to pinpoint any direct link, or lack of direct link, between board breaking and late-life osteoarthritis. Perhaps the only conclusion that can be drawn from this survey is how difficult it is to obtain enough data to draw meaningful conclusions on the subject.

[1] The authors suggested that mid-aged women were mostly in paid employment and were therefore more active than their older counterparts. Very likely the mid-aged women reported no exercise as such, yet were leading

more active lives than their older counterparts.
2. I think this is very conservative, but I have been unable to find reliable figures for the punching velocity of typical untrained people. Perhaps 8mps is more likely.
3. This is a function of transference. A downward strike could have 100%, or close to it, of body mass transferred to the striking limb. Conceivably, a person skilled in keying into the ground could even transfer more than 100% of his mass, using his feet to brace his mass against the ground, effectively transferring the ground mass into the striking limb.

References

Armenti, A. (1992). *The physics of sports*. College Park, Maryland: American Institute of Physics.

Chakravarty, E. (2008). Long distance running and knee osteoarthritis: A prospective study. *American Journal of Preventive Medicine*, 35(2): 133-138.

Cooper, C. (2003). Occupational activity and arthritis of the knee. *Annals of the Rheumatic Diseases*, 53(2): 90-93.

Currey, J. (2002). *Bones: Structure and mechanics*. Princeton, NJ: Princeton University Press.

Gelber, A. (2000). Joint injury in young adults and risk for subsequent knee and hip osteoarthritis. *Annals of Internal Medicine*, 133(5): 321-328.

Heesch, K. (2007). Relationship between physical activity and stiff or painful joints in mid-aged and older women: A 3-year prospective study. *Arthritis and Therapy*, 9: R34.

Rossignol, M. (2004). Primary osteoarthritis and occupation in the Quebec national health and social survey. *Occupational and Environmental Medicine*; 61(9): 729-735

Stevens, J. (2001) *Budo secrets: Teachings of the martial arts masters*. Boston: Shambhala Publications.

Teitz, C. (1998). Premature osteoarthritis in professional dancers. *Clinical Journal of Sports Medicine*, 8(4): 255-259.

Van der Sluis, I. (2002, October). Reference data for bone density and body composition measured with dual energy x ray absorptiometry in white children and young adults. *Archives of Disease in Childhood*, 87(4): 341-347.

Acknowledgment

Special thanks to those who helped with the photography:
Gary Wilkins, who bravely suspended the boards,
and to photographers Wally Seccombe and
Marilyn Jankowska for capturing the moments.

chapter 10

Ryukyu Kempo and Small Circle Jujitsu

by Will Higginbotham, B.A.

Where I Learned These Techniques

As a strong proponent of the value of classical kata practice, I stress that applications for techniques can be derived directly from traditional katas. Further, karate and jujutsu techniques work wonderfully well together to "fill in the gaps" in seeking ways to maintain control of an attacker.

The particular sets of techniques or "flows" presented in this chapter are variations on—and combinations of—well-known and commonly practiced individual techniques. The reason these sets are among my favorites is that they illustrate the importance of preventing the practitioner from simply "stalling out" after performing a single counter to a given attack.

The first set deals with a takedown to a prone position from a hammerlock, using a finger lock for maximum stability and control. Here I credit Leon Jay (Small Circle Jujitsu) for sharing his expertise in joint manipulation.

The second set involves a series of defenses from a right-left punch combination delivered by a determined assailant. At each step the defender aims to control his opponent and deter further aggression, using force proportionate to the nature and duration of the attack. By aiming blocks and strikes at specific pressure points, the defender hopes to injure or disable the attacking arm, stun the attacker, and finally subdue him altogether by taking him to the ground in a controlled fashion. Here I credit George Dillman (Ryukyu Kempo) for sharing his expertise with pressure-point techniques.

Memorable Incidents Involving These Techniques

The hammerlock is sometimes taught as a static technique, leaving the defender holding the attacker in a somewhat precarious standing position from which a number of counters and escapes can be performed. A common follow-up is the application of additional torque to the shoulder, forcing the opponent to the prone position on the floor. One problem with this follow-up is that the defender is often forced to slam the opponent downward in order to maintain control. The version presented here shows how the defender can maintain a higher degree of control throughout the encounter.

One of my senior students—sixth dan Anthony Everett—is the agent in charge of training on the national level for the Department of Veterans Affairs. Because of the superior control afforded by the takedown from the hammerlock presented herein, the agency has adopted this particular technique as part of its combatives training in controlling and handcuffing.

The defense for the right-left combination attack is similarly controlled, but equally powerful and adaptable. One sensible goal is to use the minimum force required to prevent the attack and keep oneself safe. This is important for ethical as well as legal reasons. In the sequence illustrating the defense against the right-left punch combination, the defender reacts to protect himself and control the situation with escalating force, making sure the response at each stage is proportionate to the increasing intensity of the attack.

This technique is also highly adaptable. For example, when working this technique with a Muay Thai stylist at a European seminar in 2008, the attacker had the good sense and training to retract his left fist to guard his jaw after I had blocked his second attack. Luckily, force can be easily transferred through a solid object, and I was able to complete the technique perfectly simply by palming the attacker's own guard into the intended target.

Tips on Practicing These Techniques

In applying the controlled takedown from the hammerlock, the free hand is used to control the shoulder, preventing the opponent from turning counter-clockwise to spin out of the hold. As the right hand slides down and behind the opponent to grasp his fingers, the left hand snakes around the elbow to create a base and prevent a spinning or turning counter to the finger lock. As the defender applies controlled pressure to the fingers, the left hand strokes the carotid sinus to force the opponent to the ground.

In the defense against the right and left punch sequence, the defender begins with a guard position that is intended to be relatively nonthreatening. When the attacker punches, the defender parries and simultaneously "stings" the sensitive points on the inside of the wrist with his other hand, so as to deter any further attack if possible. If the attacker continues with a left punch, the defender clears the parried right punch down and to the side while simultaneously parrying the incoming attack with his rising, right ridge hand. If these two defenses have not ended the confrontation, the defender is now inside the attacker's guard and has a clear shot at neck and head targets. Finally, by cupping the back of the attacker's neck with the right hand while leaving the left hand free, the defender can apply as little or as much force as is needed to take the attacker down and can control his fall to boot.

• • •

Technique 1: Controlled Takedown from the Hammerlock

1a) The defender slaps the opponent's attacking right forearm down with his left palm, then shoots his right hand across and behind the attacker's elbow. 1b) The defender continues around the forearm with his left hand and pulls with his right to rotate the opponent. He "tightens" the hammerlock by stroking the right palm up. 1c) The defender slides his right hand down and behind to grasp his opponent's ring and pinky fingers. His left hand wraps the elbow from inside to prevent twisting out of the finger lock. 1d) Once the finger lock is secure with the right hand alone, the middle finger of the left hand strokes up the sternocleidomastoid muscle, forcing the assailant to fall on his back. The reverse two-finger lock is then used to flip him over on his face, using his left hand to cup his head for safety. 1e) The defender can now base the finger lock with his leg for more intense control while kneeling on the opponent's sciatic nerve to stabilize him.

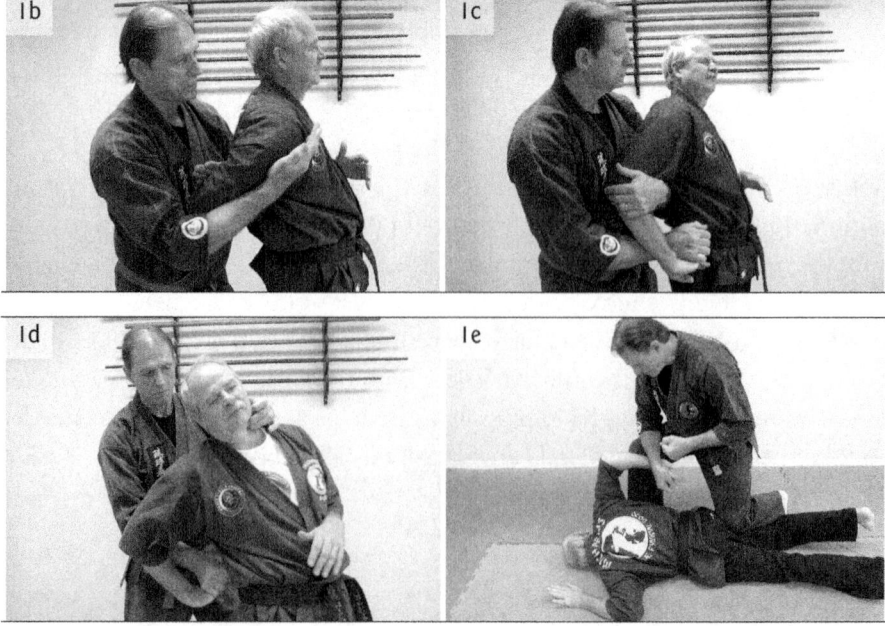

Technique 2: Escalating Defense from Right and Left Punches

2a) When confronted, the defender assumes a hands-up, palm-open "don't hurt me" type of posture. 2b) If the attacker strikes, the defender parries down with a left open-palm slap while striking to the inside of the wrist with a right punch. 2c) If the attack continues with the free left hand, the defender's parrying hand continues its arc to clear the opponent's right arm. The defender's right ridge hand parries up, striking. 2d) The defender is now inside his attacker's guard and in a position to strike simultaneously to the neck and jaw. 2e) The defender's right hand snakes around to cup the attacker's neck, while his left hand can press or strike the forehead as needed to subdue the attacker with minimum damage and maximum control.

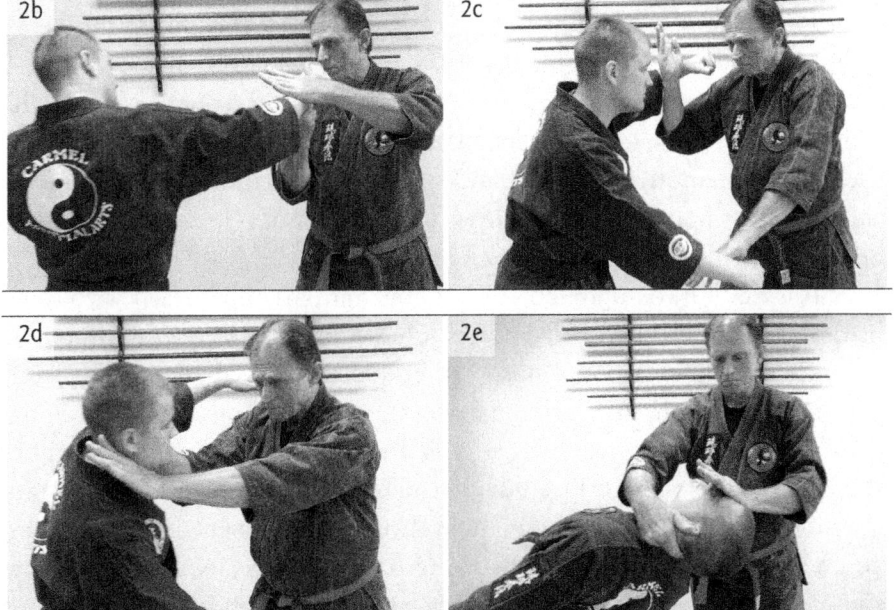

chapter 11

Kata-based Training of Goju-ryu Karate

by Marvin Labbate

This short piece presents Okinawan Goju-ryu karatedo as a kata-based training system. It brings together kata-based training elements for various levels of understanding and application, combining solo principles and partner-based training principles. At its most basic level, a kata is a form or pattern of movements that train various fighting scenarios and responses. At the most advanced level, for which katas serve as the encyclopedia of the entire martial art, katas provide a sequence of dangerous to deadly techniques. Between the two extremes are levels of development to which masters have historically controlled access. While these restrictions were to ensure that only those with appropriate moral, spiritual, and physical preparation were able to use and teach these ideas, in modern times these restrictions have been relaxed for commercial gain. Thus, it is more important than ever to address responsible training and use of these principles.

As this chapter will discuss, the art of Goju-ryu is also a system. While karate training can be "performance based" for showy applications such as tournaments, traditional training for self-defense is kata based, and thus the center of the Goju-ryu system is also kata-based training. Each series of kata movements has a translation—the basic form and pattern—but it has many applications. Thus, while "practicing" a kata provides a first step, if the karate practitioner wishes to fully grasp a kata's richness, he or she will explore these applications. Furthermore, while the understandings and applications of the kata will vary, the basic system applies to any and all katas. As I will describe below, this system includes familiarizing oneself with the background of the kata, working through solo and partner training, and developing a self-defense repertoire based on traditional kumite sets.

It is helpful to approach any kata by familiarizing oneself with some historical and technical background. One combines a general awareness of karate-related culture, philosophy, etiquette, and language with kata-specific information, such as the name of the kata, its definition or meaning, and its history or origins (such as why and how it was developed, when, where, and with whom). By studying the background of a kata, the karate practitioner gains insight that can help develop the kata and its applications. He understands that historically there have been various levels of kata application: obvious techniques; intermediate-level applications that must be taught; individual interpretations through which the black belt ranks are able to become artists; and *okuden,* or hidden techniques and principles that historically masters did not transmit except to select individuals with sufficient merit. Through this background, a kata is understood as a deep, meaningful source of martial knowledge. Then the practitioner moves on to training in the kata itself.

Kata-based training has two major components: solo and partner training. In solo training, one begins with memorizing the pattern of a kata, its basic steps and movements. Once the pattern is mastered, principles are layered over and integrated with the movements. Among others, key principles include the Sanchin kata's principles of structure, movement, and breathing, and karate drum principles of generating close-range power. Thus, the elementary movements of the kata are broken into parts that are drilled in order to internalize the basics and develop the specific kata. This layered solo training gives basic body mechanics and allows the kata to evolve. Solo movement is then further developed by moving with a partner. Partner training adds elements such as distancing, timing of entering and exiting, and awareness. This phase includes practices such as *tai sabaki* (body shifting, or giving up space without giving up ground) and *kakie* (push-hands, or sensitivity training, which teaches how the partner will move without having to watch).

In order to practice and develop kata-based training (whether novice, intermediate, or advanced) into a fighting or self-defense repertoire of techniques, one then follows a formula based on traditional sparring sets, some of which are presented here in the diagrams below. These kumite sets can include the following: basic *bunkai,* or one-step attacks with defense and counter taken from kata sequences; advanced bunkai that combine the basic moves with takedowns; flow drills that teach how to flow from one move to another with a partner; basic grappling; advanced grappling with the application of choking techniques; two-person katas; freestyle drills; and other variations. Together, these elements develop any kata at any level as an effective means of self-defense.

The steps for the kata-based training system are the same for any kata. A single step, sweep, and shuto technique—from a novice Goju-ryu kata called Gekisai-Dai-Ichi—is presented here in order to illustrate the fact that when combining the principles and formula, the basics are the best techniques. By following the system, one can defend oneself even with a basic kata. As part of individual karate practice, however, the practitioner will apply the training system to different katas based on his or her individual body, skills, and gifts.

Basic Tegumi (Grappling) Kumite

1a) The attacker and defender are in traditional grappling stances. 1b) The defender throws a right slap to the left side of the attacker's neck. 1c) The defender follows through with his right hand and sweeps the attacker's front leg.

1d) The defender throws a right shuto to the right side of the attacker's neck. 1e) The defender's arm continues around the attacker's neck, forcing him down. 1f) The defender applies a choke.

Jiyu Kumite (Freestyle Sparring)

2a) The attacker and defender pair off in sparring stances. 2b) The defender grabs the attacker's leading hand and chambers.

Acknowledgments to Greg Macedin and John Nelson for help with the demonstrations; Jill Petersen Adams, assistant; and Scott Gardner, photography.

2c) The defender steps in and sweeps the attacker's leading leg. 2d) The defender throws a shuto across the attacker's neck.

chapter 12

Tekko: Ryukyu Kobudo Shinkokai's Knuckle Duster

by Mario McKenna, M.Sc.

Where I Learned These Techniques

Most karate practitioners are familiar with the tonfa, bo, sai, and nunchaku as they are practiced in many karatedo dojos around the world, but Ryukyu Kobudo, the weapons tradition of Okinawa, encompasses a wider range of weaponry than just these four. This was the extent of my knowledge until I moved to Japan and began studying Ryukyu Kobudo formally with Minowa Katsuhiko and Yoshimura Hiroshi. Under their tutelage I learned that Ryukyu Kobudo uses a plethora of different weapons that are supported by multiple katas and two-person sets. One of those weapons I was introduced to is the *tekko*, or *tikko*, as Minowa preferred to call it.

It was during my second year of practice that I first encountered the tekko, and my initial thought was that it resembles a "knuckle duster." After being handed a pair, it was obvious that this weapon was much "meatier" than a "knuckle duster"; it was thicker, denser, and heavier—it clearly had intent. Yoshimura told me the tekko was a *kakushi buki*, or concealed weapon, that was popular for self-defense in old Okinawa, since it is relatively small and easy to conceal.

For several months I was drilled in *Maezato no tekko*, the kata that supports the techniques for the tekko. This kata is named after its creator, Minowa sensei's teacher, Taira Shinken (1897-1970). Once I had gained some proficiency with the tekko, I was slowly introduced to the two-person fighting set.

Memorable Incidents Involving These Techniques

I had been practicing both the kata and two-person set for a year and was starting to feel more comfortable with them. Along the way there were the usual mishaps, mostly self-inflicted, but not always. Yoshimura sensed my surge in confidence and, like any good teacher, decided to push the boundaries a little. The next time we practiced the two-person fighting set, he went a little harder and a little faster. Tekko in hand, I was the defender, but I struggled to keep up and it was obvious my technique wasn't good enough yet. Minowa looked over and said, "*Mada desu*"; you don't have it right yet.

A few months later I was facing Yoshimura again, but this time I was the attacker. Bo in hand, I delivered the strikes with all the vigor and stupidity of youth. A few sequences into the set, I felt a sharp pain on my fingers and dropped the bo to the floor. Yoshimura had given me a light tap with the tekko. Nothing was broken, no blood, but that light tap taught me how dangerous and debilitating this weapon can be in the proper hands. It is a lesson I never forgot.

Tips on Practicing These Techniques

Although the original two-person set has the attacker using a bo, the techniques are not limited to countering only that weapon. They can be applied equally against empty-hand attacks or bladed weapons. To that end, it is important to become accustomed to different combative engagement distances and their associated timing (*maai*). When practicing these techniques, I recommend progressing through different ranges and weapons until proficiency is reached:

❶ close range (e.g., empty hand)
❷ short range (e.g., knife or stick)
❸ midrange (e.g., four-foot staff), and
❹ long range (e.g., six-foot staff)

When using the tekko as a weapon of self-defense, there are two key points you should bear in mind. The first is to not become trapped in a block-and-counter paradigm. This is not only slow and unrealistic, but also potentially dangerous to the defender. Instead, attack and defense are to be used simultaneously. That is, the tekko must be used to strike vulnerable parts of the opponent's body as he attacks. Strikes should be aimed at the joints of the body, as this inhibits or stops the attacker from using his own weapons. The second point is that footwork (*taisabaki*) is extremely important for fist-loaded weapons like the tekko. You must not only avoid the attack, but place yourself in an advantageous position to deliver your own. The following photographs illustrate the use of the tekko against the empty hand.

• • •

Acknowledgements

I would like to extend my sincerest thanks to Maik Hassel for the fine photography work, and Brent Zarparniuk for posing as the *kosha* (opponent) in the photographs.

Technique 1: Overhead Deflection and Low Strike

1a) Face your opponent with your left foot forward in a natural stance. Both hands are in front of your torso with the left hand leading. 1b) As the opponent moves forward to punch, step forward with the right foot, and raise both hands to catch the opponent's arm at the elbow. **Key point:** *Take a deep step forward into the opponent; palms are open when performing the over-head deflection with the right hand on top of the left hand (see tekko detail).* 1c) Shift your weight onto your lead leg and press up with both palms to unbalance the opponent. **Key point:** *To clear the attack, spring the hands up and away.* 1d) Shift your weight onto your right leg, bend your torso, and strike down in front of you with both hands on the opponent's knee. **Key point:** *Use the handles of the tekko to strike the opponent. The thumbs apply pressure to the top of the tekko for stability*

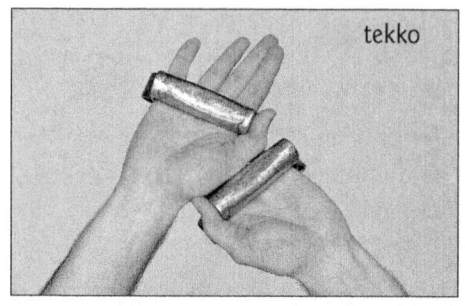

Technique 2: Midlevel Counterstrike

2a) Face your opponent with your right foot forward in a natural stance. Both hands are in front of your torso with the right hand leading. 2b) Pivot to the right, step in with your right foot and deliver a left vertical punch. **Key points:** *Shift your weight to your rear leg as you pivot; stabilize the tekko by pressing down with your thumb on top of the handle; the counterstrike is aimed at the opponent's arm (i.e., elbow, wrist, or hand—see detail shown above).* 2c) Press with the right tekko to unbalance the opponent and move his arm away. **Key point:** *When you press with the tekko make sure to do it in a snapping action.* 2d) Shift your weight onto your right leg, slide in and deliver a high, left vertical punch. **Key point:** *The punch must be performed vertically with the thumb stabilizing the tekko.*

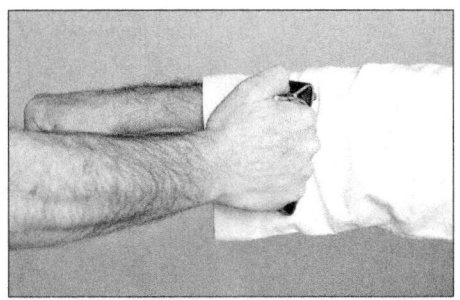

index

Adams, Hamish, 40
All-Okinawa Karate Federation, 13 note 3
Arakaki, Ryuko, 2, 76-77
Arakaki, Ankichi, 48
Arakaki Seisho, 2
Arneil, Steve, 15-46
Ashihara, Hideyuki, 29
Association for the Martial Virtues of Great
    Japan (Dai Nippon Butokukai), 3, 101
Azuma, Takashi, 41
Battle of Okinawa, 4
Bolton, Bob, 17
Bluming, Jon, 31-32
British Karate Control Commission, 39
British Kyokushinkai, 44
Bubishi, 2, 80-81, 92 note 8, 108
Chinto kata, 70
Collins, Howard, 40
Daito-ryu, 49
DeBacario, Luis, 52
Dillman, George, 64-74, 150
Donovan, Ticky, 40
Draeger, Donn, 17-18, 20, 55
Enoeda, Keinosuke, 30, 38
Fitkin, Brian, 39-40
Five Ancestors Fist, 108
Fong, Leo, 67-68, 70
forearm training (kote kitae), 86, 88-90
free-style sparring, 9, 24-26, 53
Fujian Province, 2, 77, 92 note 8
Fujihira, Akio, 29, 36-38
Funakoshi, Gichin, 13 note 4, 141
Gaviola, Frank, 53, 62 note 5
Gekisai Itchi/Ni katas, 10, 118 note 1, 155
Go Kenki (Wu Xiangui), 108-109
Gracie, Family, 11, 13 note 5,
Hanko-ryu, 2

Hanashiro, Chomo, 62 note 2
Hawai'i Karate Kodanshakai, 50
Higa, Seiko, 118 note 3
Higashionna (Higaonna), Kanryo, 76-80,
    108-109
Higgins, Billy, 40
Ishibashi, Masami, 27-29
Itosu, Yasutsune, 48
Jana, Teido, 3
Jay, Wally, 67-68, 70
Kano, Jigoro, 10, 130-131
Kanazawa, Hirokazu, 30, 40
kenjutsu, 80, 92 note 7
Kenkyukai, 105, 109
Kinjo, Hiroshi, 50, 62 note 2
Kim, Richard, 47-62
Knighton, Stan, 40
Ko Ryuru, 2, 77, 79, 108
Kodokan, 17, 31
Kojo Taitai, 2
Kurosaki, Kenji, 18, 26-27, 29, 35-38
Kururunfa kata, 1, 85, 107
Kyoda, Juhatsu, 78, 92 note 2
Kyokushin, 10, 13 note 4, 15-46, 62 note 1
Lee, Bruce, 9, 67-68, 70, 72
Mabuni, Kenwa, 105-106
Maeda, Esai, 13 note 5
Masami, Ishibashi, 27
Matayoshi, Shinpo, 84, 95, 117-118
Matusumura Sokon, 48
Meibukan, 5, 9, 12, 75-91, 133
Minowa, Katsuhiko, 158
Miyagi, Chojun, 1-5, 7-8, 62 note 3,
    76-82, 88, 91, 92 note 5, 99, 101,
    104-109, 111, 113, 117, 118 note 1
Naha-te, 2, 78, 92 note 3
Nagamine Shoshin, 118 note 1

Naihanchi kata, 66
Nakamura, Tadashi, 29-31, 33, 36, 38, 43, 45
Nakasone, Genwa, 94, 104-105
Ninomiya, Kojo, 41
Okada, Hirofumi, 28-29, 33
O'Neill, Terry, 40
100-man fight, 32-36
Oshiro, Chojo, 62 note 2
Oyama, "Mas" Masutatsu, 13 note 4, 15-22, 24-38, 43-45, 50, 62 note 1
Oyama, Shigeru, 30-31, 36, 38, 43, 45
Oyama, Yasuhiko, 36
Oyata, Seiyu, 66-67
Pai, Daniel, 68
Parker, Ed, 68
Pinan kata, 66
Poynton, Bob, 40
Presas, Remy, 67-68, 73
pressure point theory, 64-73, 136, 150
punching post, 3, 77, 81-83, 120-128,
Ricci, Brian, 50-55, 58, 60-61
rokkishu exercise, 7, 13 note 1, 108
Royama, Hatsuo, 41
Saiha/saifa kata, 27-28, 107, 111
Sampei kata, 41
Sanchin kata, 1, 3-4, 7, 10, 81, 86, 107-109, 111, 137, 155
Sanseiru kata, 85, 107, 111
Sato, Katsuko, 41
Seido style, 45
Seipai kata, 6, 84, 107, 112
Seisan kata, 4, 6, 81, 87, 107, 11
Seiunchin kata, 4, 81, 107
Shidokan, 41, 45
Shisochin kata, 107
Shinzato Jinan, 2, 4, 80, 92 note 5
Shiroma, Masahige, 78, 92 note 3
Shishochin kata, 10
Shorin-ryu, 17, 48, 92 note 3, 118 note 1

Shotokan, 17, 25, 52-53, 62 note 1
Shukokai, 25
Shuri city/castle, 4, 101-102, 107
Small Circle Jujitsu, 150
Soeno, Yoshiji, 41, 45
Soken, Hohan, 65-67, 70
spear (*yari*), 49, 55-56
staff (bo), 53, 55-61, 158
Suparinpei kata, 107, 111
Suzuki, Tatsuo, 30, 38
Taira, Shinken, 158
Takeda, Sokato, 49
tekko, 158-161
Tensho kata, 1, 4, 7, 106-113, 116-117
test breaking skills, 28, 142-149
Toguchi, Seikich, 84
toudi (China hand), 104-105
Trias, Robert, 68
Ventresca, Peter, 52
Wado-ryu, 25
Wai Xianxian, 108
Wall, Kimo, 117, 118 note 3
Wang Xiangzhai, 49
White Crane, 108, 111
Wing Chun, 108
World Union of Karate Organizations, 39-40
World War II, 4, 50, 92 note 5, 95, 117
Yabu, Kentsu, 48
Yagi, Meitatsu, 1-3, 5-6, 8, 11-12, 75-78, 81, 86-88, 91
Yagi, Meitoku, 1, 3-6, 11, 76, 80-83, 85-86, 88, 91, 91 note 1, 133
Yamaguchi, Gogen, 17-18, 27, 50, 62 note 3, 81
Yasuda, Eiji, 27
Yoshida, Kotaro, 47, 49, 56
Yoshimura, Hiroshi, 158-159
Yunigawa no kon kata, 56, 58
Zen Bei Butokukai, 50-51, 54-56

Printed in Great Britain
by Amazon